20 THINGS I WISH I HAD MASTERED BY AGE 30

FOR A LIFE OF EXCELLENCE

By
ALEXANDER GYIMAH AGYEMANG
Empowerment Series

20 Things I Wish I had mastered by age 30 for a life of excellence

© Alexander Gyimah Agyemang

First Published February, 2019

Unless otherwise stated all scripture quotations are from the New International Version of the Bible © 2011 and the King James Version of the Bible© 1987.

ISBN-:978-1095885000

All right reserved. No part of this publication may be reproduced, stored in a retrieval system, or transmitted in any form or by any means-electronic, mechanical, photocopying, recording or otherwise without prior permission from the author.

ENLIGHTENED WORD TEACHING MINISTRY

C/O Post, Office Box 783, Takoradi Western Region, Ghana / West Africa

E-mail: lexgyi@yahoo.com or lexgyi@gmail.com

Lexgyi.blogspot.com

Instagram: lexgyi

Facebook.com / lexgyi@yahoo.com

Youtube: Alexander Gyimah Agyemang

Twitter.com/LEXGYI

Published by Amazon.com,USA

Dedication

I dedicate this book to Frederick Kwabena Agyemang and Elsie Asantewah Agyemang you are the inspiration for this Book. Your lives will be a lot different if you had mastered the habits and ideas in this book by age thirty.

REVIEWS

Remarkable and insightful. A book dealing with comprehensive habits every youth needs to know. The author presents thorough guidelines on how to maximise potential habits for a life of excellence. To benefit from this book, do not read it like a story book, instead take time to study and practise the habits recommended in this book and you will experience great impact.

Until I read the manuscript, I knew little about the power of the mind and its imaginations. I now know that if I master meditation, I will become highly productive. I choose to think deep to maximise my potential.

As youth leader, leading teens and adult youth, I can confidently say that this book will shape your dream and challenge you to aim high and pursue purpose. I highly recommend this book to all youth who lay hold of it to enrich their talents.

Emmanuel Larwey (Medical Laboratory Scientist –MLS)

(Youth leader, PIWC TAKORADI)

I am Osei Sefa Kelvin. I am 25 years of age and a graduate of the Kwame Nkrumah University of Science and Technology. Currently I am a National Service Person. The empowerment series on the '15 habits I wish I had mastered before age 30 for a life of excellence' has had a great impact on me, especially concerning the identification of talents. After reading the chapter on identification of talent, I realised that I am a good teacher and writer. I will therefore pursue this so I can make great impact wherever I find myself.

Kelvin Osei Kelvin (BSc. Natural Resources Managements)

This book can be described as a self-revealing adventure series. It is well suited for any young person who seeks to live a life of purpose and focus. It is in itself a corrective tool for anyone above the age bracket mentioned, who has strayed. Its conversational and practical approach is fit for any 21st century discerning reader. The author's shared life experiences is a message for us all. Let us get ready for an exciting journey to destiny with a message that is in harmony with the messenger.

Stephen Chemel-Eghan Trained Chemist, High School Tutor and Youth Worker

ACKNOWLEGEMENT

I will like to thank Stephen Chemel-Eghan for his review of this entire book and for making several insightful suggestions.

CONTENTS	PAGE
Copyright page	.b
Dedication	.i
Reviews	.ii
Acknowledgment	.iv
Part One - Child Of The Rock	**.1**
Part Two – Power Of Habits	**6**
Part Three – Powerful Creatures Of Habits	**12**
Part Four - The Ideal Of Ages Before 30	**27**
Part Five: Why Excellence By Age 30?	**34**
Part Six	**38**
Habit 1: Appreciation of My Net Worth	38
Habit 2: Knowing How to Assess My Net Worth…………….49	

CONTENTS	PAGE
Habit 3 – The Art of Setting Goals	64
Habit 4 – Networking	72
Habit 5: Knowing Investments and Wealth Building	78
Habit 6: Leverage	87
Habit 7 – The Use of My Talent	91
Habit 8 – The Art of Marketing Or Selling	97
Habit 9 – Knowing How To Judge Character	103
Habit 10 – The Use of My Spiritual Gifts	110
Habit 11 – Knowing How to Live According To God's Purpose for Your Life	120
Habit 12 – Coding	126
Habit 13 – Self Promotion	132

CONTENTS	PAGE
Habit 14 – Reading Non Academic Books ..	137
Habit 15 – Use of Emotional Intelligence	141
Habit 16 – Memorisation of Scriptures	146
Habit 17 – The Playing Of An Instrument	151
Habit 18: The Channelling Of My Passion Into Productive Ventures	.153
Habit 19: The Art of Showing Gratitude Always	.163
Habit 20: Public Speaking	169
Decision page	.175
Other Books by Author...............	177
Bibliography	178

PART ONE: CHILD OF THE ROCK

In The Beginning

I was born in the wee hours of Sunday at the Holy family hospital under the hills of the *Odweanoma* Mountains missing my mother's birthday by just some hours. Indeed my birthday is just a day after hers: I was therefore denied nothing good since my parents were expatriates in Niger at the time. I wore designer clothes and my shoes alone were sacks full. When I returned to Ghana permanently in 1987 to stay amongst my people I made some observations quickly. I made this observations because of the vast differences in habits I saw growing up amongst a people known for their prowess in entrepreneurship in Ghana. This imposed on me unconsciously certain expectations from life. I grew up seeing the most lavish of funerals and very flamboyant celebrations like the Easter holidays.

My questions to my elders as to why a lot of our people are so rich had varied answers. Some told me it was from money rituals but the majority told me it was because they have the ability to delay gratification till they had enough to show off. This explanation made sense to me because one of our slogans as a people when loosely translated is 'Children of the Rock'. Meaning we come from struggle and so are relentless in our endeavours till we are successful. The competition amongst the various town people to put up mega mansions could be seen on many major street as you enter or exit the towns in the area. These holiday homes of people who also have mansions in the cities could easily be mistaken for three or four star hotels. Sometimes these building were just neighbours with the habitation of poor people from the same town or even extended family members. After my basic education I came to the conclusion that since the very rich people live in the same neighbourhood with the very poor then it means the rich have different habits from the poor since they were all born in the same environment.

Looking at the very richest who were not only the richest amongst our people but also in the country and studying their investments and listening to the stories of how they came to be so successful, I came to the firm conclusion that it was just habits they mastered growing up in the area. I also observed that the families which had grown to be rich over the years trained up the children to take up the same habits of the man who started the businesses which made them wealthy. In most cases the uncle will take the nephew and train him in the things he needs to learn to carry his legacy even further. The pressure to make it early so your family will also join the rich and highly respected was so strong that many of my school mates dropped out of school at the basic level to start apprenticeship under relatives doing business in the city.

At about fourteen years, I drew up my first plan to dominate the world with my businesses, giving it a name and even incorporating it to have subsidiaries. Then at age fifteen I gave my life to Christ and suddenly, I saw those ambitions as worldly and materialistic. I had the habit of setting goals and reading but I hated selling and also found self-promotion offensive. Overtime I became more introvert and lost the edge to start and grow businesses or ministries because I became content with being at the background instead of stepping up to be counted.

My desire to lead which is a crucial habit for entrepreneurs was side-lined and replaced with that for following others due to my misunderstanding of what was expected of me as a young Christian. This misunderstanding got me wondering what the way forward in the wilderness of life was. My confusion continued till my mid-thirties before I started getting re-enlightened about life and what is needed to be truly successful without compromising my believes. The very first job interview I attended I excelled so much that the panel stopped the interview at a point and then asked me a question which sent me back to my pre conversion teen's obsession with entrepreneurship. You are a kwahu they quizzed, so why are you here searching for a job when you can be an entrepreneur? The fact that people who had not seen me before attributed certain habits to me because of where I hailed from surprised me. Years after failing at this job and going on to do two other jobs with less satisfaction. I set out to read hundreds of books on finance, leadership and making generational impact. When I was through, I proceeded to the biographies of company founders and studied the start of many giant corporations in the world.

After hours of listening and watching videos on accomplished men and women from the kwahu Area and the rest of the world I came to the conclusion that, if I had mastered just twenty (20) habits I would have been a highly accomplished person before hitting my thirties in whatever endeavour I had set my mind to. I have listed these habits and explained how they could be mastered for excellence and not for riches alone. Because excelling is an attribute of God and it is good for all situations: whether tangible or intangible. If you are less than thirty years of age then good for you because your life is going to definitely change for the better even if you master just half of these habits. But if you are above thirty it is not too late because life does not start at the same age for everyone: some start in the morning and others in the night. It is always better late than never.

PART TWO: POWERFUL EFFECTS OF HABITS

Power

According to the [1]Merriam-Webster dictionary power is: *(1) a : ability to act or produce an effect b: capacity for being acted upon or undergoing an effect and c legal or official authority, capacity, or right.; (2) a: possession of control, authority, or influence over others b: one having such power; specifically: a sovereign state c: a controlling group: establishment —often used in the phrase the powers that be ;(3) a : physical might b : mental or moral efficacy c : political control or influence.*

Simply put power is the ability to effect a desired change and the right to exercise that power. The Greeks have two words for power: *dunamis and exousia.* **Dunamis** *means that power is ability or influence and* **exousia** *means authority which is the right or privilege to exercise power*[2]. Anything that has power has the ability to shape lives or influence the course of our lives. Hence the importance of knowing what has power over us as young people. We are talking about power because habits are so powerful.

To understand why habit are powerful we need to know what influences it has on our day to day lives.

Habits

Habits are the things we do unawares or things we do by default. All habits are learned. Contrary to popular opinion no one is born with a habit. Habits are not innate they are all acquired. Please get this truth: habits are not genetic! Please agree to this truth or you will never be able to change a bad habit. Habits are simply behaviours that are repeated so many times that the brain develops an autopilot system for it to happen on its own. A habit is an auto replay system that the body sets to avoid mental analysis of an action it has learned to execute several times. Many habits are formed on the blind side of the practitioners. Addictions are simply habits that you have lost control over mentally, emotionally and physically.

Wikipedia defines a habit as *a routine of behaviour that is repeated regularly and tends to occur subconsciously*[3].According to the American Journal of Psychology (1903) *a "habit, from the standpoint of psychology is a more or less fixed way of thinking, willing, or feeling acquired through previous repetition of a mental experience".* "*Habitual behaviour often goes unnoticed in persons exhibiting it, because a person does not need to engage in self-analysis when undertaking routine tasks*"[4]. *Habits are sometimes compulsory. New behaviours can become automatic through the process of habit formation*[5]. *Old habits are hard to break and new habits are hard to form because the behavioural patterns which humans repeat become imprinted in neural pathway*[6].

The Power of Habits

Habits are so powerful that they define us. If someone claims to know you: what they really mean is that they know your habits. And with that knowledge they can safely predict your actions in the future. People have been led astray because others knew their habits more than they were even conscious of themselves. Incidentally our bad habits are made known to us by our friends and relatives more than the good ones. Unless the good ones are exceptionally good and outstanding. We grew up weary of knowing almost on a daily basis how our bad habits were affecting others and why they needed to be reversed before they ruin our lives. There are basically four temperaments as described by psychologist. According to Merenda, *the four temperament theory is a proto-psychological theory that suggests that there are four fundamental personality types: sanguine, choleric, melancholic, and phlegmatic*[7].

These four basic temperaments and a combination of them alter our tendencies and hence our habits. In fact these four temperaments are a summary of the four basic habits or tendencies of people. Habits of societies become a culture and that culture then works on the new entrants to fashion them into those habits and tendencies. Understand this reader, everything you are known for is basically as a result of the habits you have exhibited or the habits of your close friends and family. So be conscious of what habits you are forming because most people will form an opinion of you through their interaction with your habits and will never give you the chance to explain yourself.

You may ask: what about the colour of our skin? Do people not judge according to the colour of our skin? That is what it may seem but racial prejudice is not necessarily because of the colour but the history associated with it. You need to know that if you allow it, other people's habits will define who you are as a person. Prejudice is having a predetermined reaction to someone because of interactions with the habits of other people like him or her. Prejudice is also another form of a bad habit acquired through years of miss-education and misinformation. So contrary to the perception that racism is because of colour, it is because mostly blacks to a racist white person is simple the summary of black behaviour or tendencies he or she has encountered or been told about. Hence his or her preconceived reaction to anyone with that skin colour.

What about where you are born? Does that not also put you in a mould in the eyes of others? Unfortunately this myth is very prevalent in people of African descent especially Sub Saharan Africans. The thought that it is where we are that defines our abilities. However, where we come from is only used to predict our habits as people from a particular location often share similar behavioural traits. Not knowing that we make our environment and not the environment making us: is why people could be leaving in paradise and still be poor. It is what you do predominantly as a person or a culture which attracts the negative tendencies of others towards you.

The powerful effects of habits is therefore all encompassing casting a shadow on everything concerning you: your skin colour;

the countries you come from or the continent you descend from and the way people of different cultures or skin tones perceive you. Every human experience is communicated through a habit or in the case of a collective group a culture. Every effort should therefore be made to develop the right habits for a life of excellence.

GOLD NUGGETS

The power of habits?

1) Power is the ability or capacity to bring about a desired outcome.

2) Habits are a routine of behaviour that is repeated regularly and tends to occur subconsciously.

3) Habits are so powerful that they define our personality and can often predict our actions.

4) Our habits and tendencies tend to cast a shadow on our skin tone and place of birth or decent.

PART THREE: POWERFUL CREATURES OF HABITS

Introduction

Habits are so pervasive in our day to day activities that we often ignore its power over our lives and the decisions we make. I am going to share with you some powerful creatures of habit which will surprise you because you have always seen them as culture or things to do with nature. Nature when it comes to human behaviour is mostly nurture. Your parents or guardian passed to you the habits they were taught when they were your age and that cycle continue till we have family nature and societal norms. See these creatures of habit as such and start the process of undoing what needs undoing, unlearning what needs unlearning and redoing the things which need redoing. Since a person's character is primarily an acquired habit it can with discipline be unlearned and a better habit adopted to produce a better character in due time.

Six Bad Creatures of Habit:

1. Breakups and Divorces

Ask anyone who has gone through a break up or divorce and he or she will point to a behaviour or habit being the cause. Mostly the habit is so unbearable but the partner seem unable or unwilling to stop. The offended party will initially start to adjust to the other person till it becomes unbearable for him or her to stay in the relationship. The difficulty with bad behaviour is that it is usually done unconsciously after years of repetition. If offending parties will see their behaviour as a habit that can be unlearned instead of thinking it is a character they were born with, many relationships will be saved. A bad person is simply a person whose good habits are far outweighed by their bad habits. No bad person is thoroughly bad without one good habit.

That is why no bad person is beyond redemption. The worst of people have been transformed by the word of God and now primarily exhibit good habits. Some of these former societal misfits are now celebrated examples of outstanding people in society. People's habits become more pronounced the closer you interact with them and especially over a long period of time. I am a court connected alternative disputes resolution practitioner and all the disputes I settle between couples are all products of bad habits. Once I manage to point the offending parties back to the habit that led to the dispute they move from their entrenched positions and become ready to resolve the dispute. Law firm JMW Solicitors, which deals with over 300 divorces each year, has revealed that *one in ten cases are linked to a partner's habits*[8].

2 Obesity

Obesity is one of the powerful creatures of habits. *Worldwide obesity has nearly tripled since 1975.In 2016, more than 1.9 billion adults, 18 years and older, were overweight. Of these over 650 million were obese.39% of adults aged 18 years and over were overweight in 2016, and 13% were obese. Most of the world's population live in countries where overweight and obesity kills more people than underweight. 41 million children under the age of 5 were overweight or obese in 2016. Over 340 million children and adolescents aged 5-19 were overweight or obese in 2016* (WHO, 2018)[9].

The world has never been this obese in all of human history! Why have we become this obese? The answer is simply because our lifestyle has changed. Our habits have changed. Many people who are able to overcome obesity are people who accept that their habits have caused it and take steps to change the habit that led them there. Please stop blaming your obesity on other people or on the fact that you have low metabolism. Just change the bad habits causing it now!

Obesity among young adults is a growing problem in the United States and is related to unhealthy lifestyle habits such as high caloric intake and inadequate exercise. Accurate assessment of lifestyle habits across obesity stages is important for informing age-specific intervention strategies to prevent and reduce obesity progression (Nurs Health Sci).[10] *According to healthassist there 14 Habits That Make You Obese and Overweight : TV Watching; Eating Too Fast; Task snacking; Passion for Fast Food; Eating To Manage Feelings; Too Busy To Exercise; Your Friends Can Make You Obese; Lack Of Sleep; Missing Meal; Uncomfortable Clothing; Neglecting Scales and Boredom*[11]

Six Bad Creatures of Habit:

3 Addictions

Addictions do not only include physical things we consume, such as drugs or alcohol, but may include virtually anything, such abstract things as gambling to seemingly harmless products, such as chocolate - in other words, addiction may refer to a substance dependence (e.g. drug addiction) or behavioural addiction (e.g. gambling addiction)[12].

All addictions are products of habits. Depending on your make up and emotional maturity you can get addicted to almost anything. Believe it or not there is even one woman I watched who was seeking deliverance from addiction to finding scriptures before she took any action in her life including when to let the husband have access to her body. She could not even step out to work unless the portion of scripture she opened told her to do so. Addictions are just habits on steroids, they might not be bad habits in themselves but habits that you cannot control when and how they are done. Addictions are simply habits which are out of control and have begun to negatively impact the life of the addict.

According to Jaffe, substance use often begins as a simple rewarded experience, which through repetition and the rewiring of the brain's learning and reward circuits can become habitual. If that habit escalates into problematic substance use, we can end up with something that our society has called "addiction."[13]

There are many people occupying sensitive positions in life who are still addicted to habits which if exposed will ruin all they have built for decades. These people have not been able to overcome the addiction because they refuse to accept the fact that their bad habits led them there. These people blame all kinds of things both physical and spiritual for their addiction but refuse to accept that it took a habit to get there and so they need another powerful habit to break the cycle of addiction. No addiction just leaves on its own because it takes over the mind and sometimes even the body till if not checked it destroys and kills the addict. Addictions are another powerful consequence of habits.

Six Bad Creatures of Habit:

4 Poverty

I know people are very sensitive to other people telling them that they are responsible for their poverty. Because one of the commonest habits of the poor is that they never take responsibility for their lives. Poor people in spite of their colour believe generally that some other person is responsible for pulling them out of poverty. In any society where other groups are prevented for years from making their own decisions through slavery or servitude that group even after many years of freedom are still largely poor. Because the greatest antidote to poverty is the idea that everyone is responsible for his or her own life. So poverty has no colour or relation but a set of habits and beliefs.

A poor country or group has the same characteristics irrespective of where you find them in the world. In any poor country or neighbourhood you find excess filth, absentee fathers, crime, and lots of children per mother, poor infrastructure, and general lack of data on important social indicators and so on. No one escapes poverty by waiting for another person to work it out for him. Go to poor countries and neighbourhoods and they are always talking about how government can make their life better. People in such places are quick to make money irrespective of who gets hurt; and most people with poverty inducing habits lose millions when they are lucky to get money through sports or gambling.

Poverty inducing habits includes: living to please others, spending more money on consumption than education, no interest in reading, thinking only short term when it comes to planning, spending hours watching others on TV, not having delayed gratification and so on. These are the habits progressive countries design policies to tackle for economic growth and poverty eradication. The culture of my country taught me that, being rich happens to you, it is not something you actively pursue. So I pondered on why my tribesmen were disproportionately rich in my country. I wondered why it was happening to them more often than others. Until I read the book 'Rich Dad Poor Dad by Robert Kiyosaki', that I understood that it was because of certain habits of industry and entrepreneurship that they practiced more than others in the general population. I then resolved to never be poor in my life and adopted the habits of the rich and discontinued those of the poor in my life. For me being worthy is being healthy. Wealth needs only the grace of God, a compelling vision and time to build it.

5 Crime

I believe bad habits and crime are strongly correlated. Bad habits do not necessarily become crime but bad habits escalates to crime. That is why police officers can tell you what crime happens the most in which areas of the city. There are families where most of the males are in jail. There are whole neighbourhoods in the USA where every family has a member or more in prison. You would have thought that the next generation having lived without their fathers for most of their life would make better choices. But they pick the same habits from the neighbourhood and end up becoming just like the father they disliked so much.

Crimes are simply habits which break the law of a country. There are people who spend most of their adult life in prison because the crimes they commit are bad habits that if they do not change will keep recurring till they die. The desire for quick money, inability to control ones temper, uncontrolled lust etc. are all habits which lead to criminal conduct.

6 Mediocrity

Just as excellence is a habit mediocrity is also the product of a habit. Remember the many times you were told not to aim too high because you do not come from a privilege background. Recall the many times you were told not to do something because of your gender: because it is mainly done by people of the other gender. The tendency to assign someone to a particular fate in life because it has happened to people of similar disposition is a bad habit which forces people to accept below par performance.

I attended a public basic school in a small town. This condition was enough to make teachers and parents alike assume I could not compete with the best students in the country. I remember a friend choosing the best secondary school at the time before we wrote our basic education exams. Our own teachers called him and spent more than an hour dissuading him to choose the sixth best school in the country because the best one is too risky. What baffled us at the time was the fact that a senior of ours had made it to that school a year ahead of us. Under performance runs through societies not because of a genetic disposition but because it is taught and pass down from generation to generation.

This friend of mine accepted the advice and changed the school to the one recommended by the teachers. When the result came he had excellent in eleven out of the twelve subjects. He had passed so well he was in the best one percent of the entire graduating class that year. His desire to excel dwindled after he was denied that opportunity. I went to secondary school and university with him and saw the once best student in our year group becoming average with each passing year. The role of guardians and parents is not to use their limits as a barrier for the next generation but to push them to do better than them.

Check every failing society and you will realise that the prevailing mantra there is that the past was better than the present. The very things which brought them to mediocrity they praise in the present, because the current generation cannot go to the past to verify. As an African proverb goes *'if you did not hear it raining then you should have known when you came out of the house after the rain and found the entire surroundings wet.'* Ask the average Chinese about life and he or she will tell you that these days are better than the past. That is the habit of a society which is advancing and going places.

Two Good Creatures of Habits:

1 Language and Accent

One of the most interesting products of habits is language and the accents within the same language or dialect. I am sure you never heard anyone say that language is a habit. Well it is, because every word you know in your native tongue and any second language you know was learned. Including the pronunciation and where and when to use expressions. The phrase 'mother tongue' clearly tells us that we learnt our native language and acquired the accent of our official language from the parent or guardian who raised us.

Language is a habit we acquired from the people we interacted with as we were growing up, thus why in the same country, different communities use different accents and slangs for the same language. No one is born with an accent. Most of the time we spend in learning a language is on how to pronounce words. What is the relevance of this? The way a person speaks does not make the person. Never let anyone look down on you because of how he or she speaks. It is just a habit acquired from where the person grew up or where he or she was raised. This is the secret behind children's ability to pick languages so fast. Children have formed the habit of learning new things all the time, including a language or two and are even open to learn about five languages at a time because they see then as just acquiring new habits.

Adults are usually very slow at picking languages because we are fixated on picking the right pronunciation or the right grammar. Indeed many adults speak other languages using the pronunciations and rules of their mother tongue. This confirms that language is indeed an acquired habit that we cannot even seem to drop when speaking another. Language is not the best predictor of the speaker's knowledge of the culture of the area though he may share their accent. However for many in the developing word a British or American accent means intelligence. Forgetting the language you know already, coupled with patience and determination you can learn any language you want. After all, it is just like acquiring another habit to enable you succeed in life.

2 Praying at Set Times in a Day

Praying at set times of the day is a habit of many people around the world. My mom used to be an expatriate teaching English in the country of Niger and she told me that several times as they travelled on the high ways there, the driver will stop unfailingly to pray at set times in the day. The driver often stopped in the middle of nowhere to pray by the road side. Like an addiction they had to pray no matter how inconvenient it made the non-Muslim passengers waiting in the bus. Daniel prayed three Times in a Day without fail towards Jerusalem for decades in the kingdom of Babylon. It was a habit he could not stop even after it had become a crime punishable by death.

Now when Daniel learned that the decree had been published, he went home to his upstairs room where the windows opened toward Jerusalem. Three times a day he got down on his knees and prayed, giving thanks to his God, just as he had done before (Daniel 6:10).

Jesus had a habit of going to lonely places to pray. His secret habit of prayer is what accounted for the awesome power he displayed in public. Jesus often got up early in the morning before dawn.

But Jesus often withdrew to lonely places and prayed (Luke 5:16).

The whole nations of Israel had set times for prayer during which every self-respecting Jew went to the synagogues for prayer. It was such a habit that everyone no matter their heart went for prayer during those times.

One day Peter and John were going up to the temple at the time of prayer—at three in the afternoon (Acts 3:1)

Now that we have learnt about habits and the power they have over our tendencies, let us now consider why we need to develop these winning habits before no other age than age thirty in the next chapter.

GOLD NUGGETS

Powerful Creatures of Habits

1) Many vices which plague mankind today are creatures of habits.

2) Many people are carrying burdens which can changed if they will be prepared to unlearn the habit which led them to that situation instead of blaming others.

3) Habits control more than ninety percent of the things we do in a day.

4) Powerful habits have produced many consequences which plague the word today and need a reversal or replacement habit to undo them.

PART FOUR: THE IDEAL OF AGES BEFORE 30

Ideal Ages for Habit Mastery

The idealism of the ages before thirty: these are ages where most people have the strength of mind and body to pursue their convictions. These are the ages where people are so passionate about their heritage and are prepared to lay their lives for it. This is the time when people join armies and revolutionary groups to fight for their nation or community. It is within these ages where people complete their schooling, start work, start ministries and businesses. Most people discover the wealth of their talent during these ages before thirty.

Sports

Almost all those who are in sports and have achieved fame and success reached their peak before thirty. For most sports if you do not reach peak of your career before thirty years forget it: it will be considered too late for you to make any meaningful impact. The need to know what you are good at before age thirty is so important for those involved in sports because it involves a lot of strength and passion.

Generally speaking, athletes start to see physical declines at age 26, give or take. (This would seem in line with the long-standing notion in baseball that players tend to hit their peak anywhere from ages 27 to 30. For setting world records in a given athletic

discipline, the mean age is 26.1, so all you sports-minded thirty-something hoping to still see your name published in the Guinness Book of records may have already missed your mark.27 to 30.) For swimmers, the news is more sobering, as the mean peak age is 21(Wired, 2011)[14].

Entertainment

Entertainers have longevity somehow, especially the kind that requires less vigour but to make great impact in this industry you should already be making waves before you hit age thirty especially if you are a female artiste. Because apart from talents, looks are the most desired trait in show business. Funs and producers are fixated on the appearance of stars and expect the star to look very attractive all the time. Hence the ideal of ages before thirty. *After thirty many Hollywood stars engage plastic surgeons and other medical experts to help restore or maintain the under thirty looks. Early in their careers, WOMEN receive more movie roles than MEN. That trend reverses sharply after age 30 as men continue to receive an increasing number of roles through age 46 while women receive fewer and fewer* (Time, 2017)[15].

Marriages

Contrary to the notion that you need to marry after thirty because by then you would have experimented enough to know who the right partner is; that behaviour rather tends to make you less committed. Some even argue that both male and female would be more financially balanced for an equal relationship between husband and wife. But such people have the luxury of time because their moral upbringing tells them that marriage is like a business start-up that you can try any aspect of it till you gather enough traction for take-off.

You can easily wait to marry after thirty if you believe engaging in premarital sex is not a sin against God. Why am I saying this? Because you are the peak of your sexual desire as a men and the peak of your beauty for women in your late teen till your twenties. Most people finished universities way before thirty, how many unmarried graduates are virgins? Marriages of our parents and grandparents which succeeded for decades: especially for more than four decades are marriages where at least the wife was below thirty and the husband at most thirty years. Marrying early is good for many health and wealth creation reasons. The ages below thirty are full of strong will which can bring about a lot of conflicts between couples but they are also the ages for great accommodation of change. Marrying before thirty gives room for you to learn from your mistakes without the pressures of sickness and childbearing.

Education

Anyone who can obtain mastery in their field of studies example, attain PhD in a field of study before thirty will go places. Not knowing which way you are going academically will delay many career prospects in your life. In many universities a 25 year old and above prospective students is called a matured student because in the wisdom of the school you are coming in late. In many places around the world first degree is finished by age twenty one or twenty two. You then have nine to eight years to find yourself after your studies. Check noble laureates and great inventors around the world and you will notice one fundamental thing. They were focused on what made them great before age thirty. So before they became world renowned scientist or inventor they had years to perfect their theories and inventions. A nation which has nothing for it's under thirties to direct their energies is a nation marching into poverty and destruction.

Ministry

Jesus of Nazareth started his ministry at age thirty but before age thirty he grew in wisdom and the fear of the Lord. You do not grow in wisdom mentally neither do you grow in favour by doing nothing. So Jesus actively studied and undertook activities which brought more grace upon Him before His father in heaven and the people in His community.

And Jesus grew in wisdom and stature, and in favour with God and man

(Luke 2:52).

Jesus from the age of 12 after his Jewish ceremony to transition into manhood remained in the temple of God whilst all others His age including relatives and friends were eager to get home. Jesus saw the temple as his home and was comfortable to remain there without His parents for three solid days. Indeed Jesus was surprised His parents did not think of His father's house before searching at fun places for teens? I am asking dear reader, where would you have been found if your parents lost you for three days at the age of twelve after church service? Will a church be one of the places you are likely to be found?

After three days they found him in the temple courts, sitting among the teachers, listening to them and asking them questions. Everyone who heard him was amazed at his understanding and his answers. When his parents saw him, they were astonished. His mother said to him, "Son, why have you treated us like this? Your father and I have been anxiously searching for you." "Why were you searching for me?" he asked. "Didn't you know I had to be in my Father's house? (Luke 2: 46- 49)"

Please do not turn 30 years before you are associated with the father in heaven: find favour with God and men before you turn thirty. Develop the habit of showing wisdom in all you do and by thirty you will be already established in your society and ready to do what the lord brought you to this world to do. Let us go to the next chapter which is eager to show you the role of excellence in having a fulfilled life in spite of all the difficulties life throws at us.

GOLD NUGGETS

The ideal of ages before 30

1) The ages before thirty are full of passion and strength.
2) The ages before thirty are ages of strong conviction and accommodation for change.
3) The ages before thirty are the ages where you gain favour with God and with men.
4) The ideal age for you to prepare for a life of innovation and discovery is before you thirty years.

PART FIVE: WHY EXCELLENCE BY AGE 30?

God is Excellent

O Lord, our Lord, how excellent is thy name in all the earth! who hast set thy glory above the heavens. Out of the mouth of babes and sucklings hast thou ordained strength because of thine enemies, that thou mightest still the enemy and the avenger. When I consider thy heavens, the work of thy fingers, the moon and the stars, which thou hast ordained (Psalm 8:1-3).

Excellent is God's very nature and he demonstrates it all the time and in all he does. Excellence is not just doing better than others. Excellence is doing things the way it was originally intended. Excellence is a standard: God's own standard of how things should be done. Perfection is a form of excellence because it describes how to follow God's instruction flawlessly. Excellence therefore invokes glory because it depicts the way the creator meant it to be. Excellence should therefore be the product of mastery of a habit after much trial and correction.

Due to man's depravity after our fall from grace average performance or approach to things has become the normal way of doing things and excellence has become a rarity. Excellence has come to also mean having the highest score out of an assigned mark. Achieving excellence is conferred on the student who achieves the highest score there is in an exercise.

Excellence is a habit

Excellence is the standard for the best that a human being can achieve by way of study and practice. Excellence is never a state that you wait to get to but a skill or habit you work at mastering early in life. Hence the need to work at it at a time when you have the strength for endurance and a brain that is ready to learn new things. It is truly difficult teaching an old dog new tricks. Making adjustments in the way we think and adopting healthy habits is easier before age thirty than after. Hence the need to master healthy habits before thirty. There are many examples of this around the world in entertainment, sports, and academia, ministry where people started working on their craft before age thirty and have become icons of society. There is a reason you have so much aspiration and drive in your teens and twenties: they are meant to push you to overcome the difficulties needed to master the great habits for excellence. So a person can have an excellent spirit but no one is born excellent at any habit or skill. Mastery is always needed to become excellent at anything.

Next Generation

Out of the mouth of babes and sucklings hast thou ordained strength because of thine enemies (Psalm 8:2).

Clearly after Psalm eight verse one had talked about God's excellent name and He setting His glory above the heavens proceeds to set measures for demonstrating this glory on earth. That it is in the mouth of babes or the young has the Lord made this excellence available to silence the enemies of progress. No country which wants to excel at anything waits till it youth are matured adults before it trains them to be excellent in their professions. Excellence is needed if young people will make substantial impact on their generation and generations unborn. *There is an African proverb which says that if a game will be entertaining it will show right from the start.*

The next chapter will talk about the first habit to adopt and master before you turn 30 years of age.

GOLD NUGGETS

Why excellence by age 30?

1 The ages before thirty have a balance of strength and knowledge which is needed for difficult adjustments.

2 God is excellent by nature: His very name is excellent.

3 Excellence is something that is done habitually and not something done once in a blue moon.

4 Excellence involves mastery of a desirable habit to achieve greatness.

5 The pursuit of greatness should therefore start way before thirty years to enhance effectiveness.

PART SIX

HABIT 1: APPRECIATION OF MY WORTH

Complexity of the human body

Whilst growing up my focus on this wonderful body God has given me was to get a few more inches added to where my height reached. As a young man my idea of a wife was one who will literally 'look up' to me instead of look with me or 'look down on me'. Dear reader, observe that the 'look up' phrase in the English language is reinforcing the notion that to be taller is the same as being superior. So 'behind a successful man is a woman' another very well-known backward phrase in the English language which perpetuates notions of a bygone era. Remember all the great features you have as a young person and keep far away from anyone who is obsessed with only what is wrong with your body. Let me show you some of the incredible things your body is doing: you are truly wonderfully made.

20 THINGS I WISH I HAS MASTERED BY AGE 30 FOR A LIFE OF EXCELLENCE

I praise you because I am fearfully and wonderfully made; your works are wonderful, I know that full well (Psalm 139:14).

I hope you are not amongst the young men or women who is not happy in your skin? I promise you that after you have been exposed to how sophisticated your body is and the great things it does for you unawares every day you will agree with the psalmist that you are indeed wonderfully made.

Approximately 50,000 cells in your body will die and be replaced with new cells during the time it takes you to read this sentence. We make a new skeleton every three months and a new layer of skin every month. There's something unique about all of us, and it's not just your fingerprint. Every human has a unique tongue print, too. Every square inch of your skin contains 20 feet of blood vessels, 4 yards of nerve fibres, 1,300 nerve cells, 100 sweat glands, and 3 million cells. In one hour, your heart produces enough energy to raise a ton of steel 3 feet off the ground. You use an average of 43 muscles in your face when you frown. It only takes 17 muscles to smile. Red blood cells are frequent fliers. After being created inside the bones, the cells make approximately 250,000 round trips -- at 60,000 miles each trip-- through the body before returning to the bone marrow to die 120 days later (Martha Stewart show, 2007)[16].

The adult human body comprises 206 bones, and more than half are accounted for in the hands and feet. The heart will beat an average of 3 billion times during an average person's lifetime. The aorta is the large artery that runs down the centre of your body. It's almost the diameter of a garden hose. By contrast, capillaries, the body's smallest blood vessels, are so small that it takes 10 of them side by side to equal the thickness of one strand of human hair. The average person will lose 100 strands of hair per day and over 10 billion skin flakes. The human eye can distinguish up to a million different colours and take in more information than the largest telescope known to man. When we touch something, the signal travels through the nerves to our brain at a speed of 124 mph. The skin is the body's largest organ, but it's also a pretty big medicine cabinet. The skin secretes antibacterial substances and serves as the first layer of defence for invading microorganisms. Most bacteria that land on the skin die quickly (Martha Stewart show, 2007)[17].

An adult stomach can hold up to 1.5 litres of material, but this doesn't mean you have to test that limit at every meal. Fingernails and hair are made out of the same substance -- keratin. During the first month of life, an infant is learning so many new things that the number of connections, called synapses, between brain cells increases from 50 trillion to 1 quadrillion. By comparison, if the rest of the infant's body responded with equally rapid growth, she'd weigh 170 pounds by the time she was a month old. The big toe is one of the most important structural parts of the body. That one appendage is responsible for helping us maintain our balance and propel us forward when walking. The human liver is responsible for more than 500 distinct processes in the body. It is so important that if a person has two-thirds of their liver removed as a result of trauma or surgery, it will grow back to its original size in as little as four weeks. Beards are the fastest growing hairs on the human body. If the average man never trimmed his beard, it would grow to nearly 30 feet long in his lifetime. The average person takes 23,000 breaths a day. (Martha Stewart show, 2007)[17].

The uniqueness of the individual

Even though humans are more than seven billion on this earth our creator has made each of us unique in many ways. This he did to show that two people are never the same.

We are unique because each of us is born to make his or her own imprint on history. Combine habits of how we walk, write, knock and even sit are all so unique that they can be used to safely identify us. There are body features which are also unique: DNA, Iris, Facial uniqueness, Dental uniqueness, Voice recognition, and unique palm lines and so on.

While you may be familiar with security that employs fingerprints, voice, and retinas, the shape of your ear is just as distinguishing as your fingerprints; no two ears, even on the same person, are alike. *The way you sit—can be used to identify you. Authentication via parts of the eye, like the retina or iris, has been around for a while, but an Israeli company wants to use the unique movements of your eyes to identify you. Your nose is distinct—probably belonging to one of six common nose types—and is unlikely to be mistaken for anybody else's .Vein matching, on the other hand, can also use a finger or a palm, but provides a few additional benefits—most notably that the veins must be from a living person in order to work, and that they're very hard to fake. Your distinct body odour—and we're making no judgments here—can be used to identify you* (Moren, 2014)[18].

The Price of a Soul

*For you know that it was not with perishable things such as silver or gold that you were redeemed from the empty way of life handed down to you from your ancestors, but with the precious blood of Christ, a lamb without blemish or defect (*1Peter 1: 18-19*).*

A human being is so precious that it took the son of God to be a worthy ransom for us. Before the eyes of the creator the whole world minus all the human beings is less valuable when compared to the value of a soul. As a young person be fully persuaded of your worth no matter your colour or gender. Let no one buy your dignity with promotion or money. Always leave a room, relationship or deal with your reputation intact. You will be denied many things in the beginning but in the end your uniqueness will become evident to all.

The power of the human mind

Make use of your mind. Master the use of your imagination before the age of thirty. Every product you see around you is the product of the mind.

Now to him who is able to do immeasurably more than all we ask or imagine, according *to his power that is at work within us (*Ephesians 3:20*).*

The Lord said, "If as one people speaking the same language they have begun to do this, then nothing they plan to do will be impossible for them (Genesis 11:6*).*

As you go through school and work you will succeed in many things you attempt but fail in many others too. In fact if you are not failing at anything, then you are not trying hard enough. Spend time to imagine great things you can do; great places you can be and great people you can meet. Be inspired by your imagination and the plans you put in place to bring them into the realm of reality. Master the art of meditating on difficult situations or challenging things till your mind comes up with workable solutions. In any society the people with the most fertile of imagination lead in artistic expression, strategic policy formulation and in coming out with solutions which boost the productivity of companies. Your imagination is so powerful that if you focus it on the desires of the flesh you will be caught in its pull and fall for the consequence of following through with it destructive suggestions. Always think on things which are praise worthy and of great repute.

Every human is alive for a purpose

Then God said, "Let us make mankind in our image, in our likeness, so that they may rule over the fish in the sea and the birds in the sky, over the livestock and all the wild animals, [a] and over all the creatures that move along the ground (Genesis 1: 26)"

Man was created after God had set a purpose for His creation. He was to manage all that God had made and make his own imprint on what had been made. Man was to rule his environment and not for his circumstance to rule over him. Man already had a purpose waiting for him before he came into this world. Anyone aimless and clueless in life is a soul that has lost its fundamental reason for living: because every man or woman whether he or she knows it or not has a vision and mission for his or her life. Every man pursues what his profession or culture thrust upon him for survival or dignity till he finds his true calling in life. A man becomes a self-contain dynamo of strength and skill ready to accomplish his mission on earth when his work aligns with what his maker made him for. In fact success at anything is not because of what you do but why you do it. Purpose is a container which delivers wisdom at its best in every stage of life. You are wise because you have put to purposeful use the knowledge acquired throughout your life.

"*Before I formed you in the womb I knew[a] you, before you were born I set you apart; I appointed you as a prophet to the nations* (Jeremiah 1:5)."

You may say that the above scripture was written to Jeremiah but you will be wrong because the Bible is an example to all mankind: teaching us to live the life that our maker chose for us. Say to yourself: 'I was set apart before I was born and I was appointed to be of service to the nations.' That is clearly written in the owner's manual: the Bible. It has been proven that people live longer after experiencing famines than those of similar demographics who have not. How come the one who was deprived of some of the best foods for a long time rather becomes healthier than the one who has always had it? The answer is purpose: the body after being deprived of something as essential as food develops a keen sense of purpose, because without that sharp instinct to find and store food you would not make it in a situation of famine. People after surviving such a traumatic episode in their lives become so purposeful that they adopt habits which help them to live long to fulfil their purpose on earth.

Any country or culture where people are made to feel they have no purpose, suicide rates are very high irrespective of how rich the society is. In places where food and shelter is a matter of life and death people commit less suicides because people are consumed with the purpose of staying alive. In countries where the 'have not's are not desperately poor but feel they have nothing to contribute to society, suicides rates are much higher e.g. Japan. This also explains why there are relatively less suicides during wars than at peace times. Because during a war you are either doing the killing for your course or helping save yourself and others from getting killed: your purpose is to destroy your enemies or stay alive.

Never go through life with the attitude of always dodging purpose or work when it is assigned to you. For everyone in society finds his or her power or honour from his purpose. A king or president is served because of his or her purpose or role in the society. Serve your purpose in life and your self-worth will sky rocket before your eyes and that of your society. Train yourself to be important by fulfilling a need that is shared by many people or even the elite of that society and your worth will become evident to all. After mastering the habit of seeing yourself as one in a billion and using your unique abilities to fulfil a God given purpose you need to acquire other habits to become a man or woman of excellence. Let us go to the next chapter to see what else to master.

GOLD NUGGETS

Appreciation of my worth

1) There is only one me amongst over seven billion others.
2) My body is such a complex machine that it does trillion things without my mental input.
3) I need to develop the skill of thinking through difficulties to find solutions instead of worrying.
4) I need to channel my imagination to produce inventions which will help move society forward.
5) I need to find and pursue my purpose for being here because in it will I find relevance and true fulfilment in life.

HABIT 2: KNOWING HOW TO ASSESS MY NET WORTH

Introduction

What is net worth? Is it how much your person is worth? No! Net worth is really what you own in this world without any debts. This expression is very common in developed countries but mostly unknown to the average person in most developing ones. Your Net Worth is your financial report card. It is a measure of all you owe as against all you own. Indeed it is the value of all you own minus all that you owe. The net results of this equations is the 'net' worth. That is your worth in terms of finances after all your debts have been paid for. So net worth is not only for companies and very rich people but for everyone. The patriarchs had records of all they own and knew when they wear worthy and when they were lacking. Unfortunately most adults and youth of today do not know their net worth hence they do not know how to manage the things they buy and often end up broke, frustrated and or bitter.

Debts

Let no debt remain outstanding, except the continuing debt to love one another, for whoever loves others has fulfilled the law (Romans 13:8).

There are many people who underestimate the role of debt in a man's life. There is a reason the most modern of sky scrapers around the world have something to do with financial institutions whose main stay is the selling of debt. In fact the entire economy of this world runs primarily on debt. The world currency or money is created by banks through debt. That is why when there is no credit: borrowing from the banks, the economy gets on its knees. For currency is a creation of debt: the interest put on the money you borrow creates that amount from thin air. Debt therefore 'hires' you to create that interest in addition to the principal amount for the lender. This extra money over the amount you borrowed from the bank becomes additional money for them (bank) to lend to others to make more money.

When you start work or sometimes it may even happen earlier in the tertiary or post-secondary institutions you attend, you will be confronted with the phenomenon of using product or services today and paying later. Banks and other financial institutions will sell to you the great life on borrowed money but beware the borrower is indeed servant to the lender. Be careful of borrowing for consumption: especially in a high interest economy. You will be introduced to the habit of spending money you have not yet earned. You need to have a healthy attitude towards debts before it ruins or limits you before you are thirty years.

Do not be one who shakes hands in pledge or puts up security for debts; if you lack the means to pay, your very bed will be snatched from under you (Proverbs 22:26-27).

Be careful spending monies with the view of paying back sometime in the future. There are many graduates in the United States whose students' loan debts are so huge that it has even affected their eligibility for some types of employment. The burden of this huge loan before they even gain employment has drained the energy of their youth out of them before they hit their peak in their careers. When I finally got a stable job after school, I found to my shock that my students' loan had ballooned to a figure more than my annual salary and was compounding at a rate of 10% every year. The little money I took to cushion myself during my university education was threatening my financial future so much that I had to use my social security contributions at the time of about two years to clear it after paying to release a guarantor to take her retirement benefits. There are colleagues of mine who have not bothered to check on that little debt they took in school and may have it deducted from their retirement benefit at the time they need the money most.

Be careful when someone ask you to guarantee a loan for him or her, it may be the cause of your financial down fall. There are many people who treat debt as income: that fundamental error in judgement has killed the businesses of many up and coming business man or woman. Be careful whenever you are asked to bring family home as collateral for a facility to expand a business or improve the capacity of a business. You may control stocks or production but you do not control sale to be sure you can get the loan back with interest.

Using other peoples' money works where there is a guaranteed return which is bigger than the principal amount and interest borrowed. Even in that situation you will need to take an insurance policy to protect the goods or service from the effects of 'acts of God' to ensure the money borrowed is not lot in a natural disaster. Youth who have mastered how to use the financial system have become a delight to their families and nations. Always remember to keep an accurate record of your liabilities or debts and consciously put a strategy to pay it down till it is cleared. Always state the debts you have incurred to produce the turnover you are declaring as an individual, family or business.

This habit of periodically updating your debt profile will always keep you grounded and check you from going on a spending spree after some business or career success.

Income

Stay there, eating and drinking whatever they give you, for the worker deserves his wages. Do not move around from house to house (Luke 10:7).

I believe you have heard or read the story of Jacob and his undying love for Rachel: that he served her father for fourteen years to get the opportunity to marry her and those years seems to be days to him. Oh! The power of young love. However you may revise this Hollywood version of this love story after you have become aware of Jacobs complaints of being cheated during this period too. He was never unaware of the years passing by as was initially thought. He complained he was not given a good deal by his uncle. So much for him being overcome with Rachel's love that he was blind to being cheated story that we often associate with this part of his life. The story of young people neglecting pay for the fun of work or for the opportunity to gain relevant experience abound. Remember though a workman deserves his wages: always seek to impress early wherever you are put to gain favour for the payment of wages. All like Jacob after sometime you will add it to the reasons you are frustrated in life and may be pushed to ungodly opportunities to keep body and soul together.

Jacob said to him, "You know how I have worked for you and how your livestock has fared under my care. The little you had before I came has increased greatly, and the Lord has blessed you wherever I have been. But now, when may I do something for my own household?" "What shall I give you?" he asked. "Don't give me anything," Jacob replied. "But if you will do this one thing for me, I will go on tending your flocks and watching over them: Let me go through all your flocks today and remove from them every speckled or spotted sheep, every dark-colored lamb and every spotted or speckled goat. They will be my wages (Genesis 30:29-32,NKJV).[19]

Jacob was cheated for fourteen years till he finally gathered the courage to ask for his wages. After this his employer who before this time had convinced himself that each of his daughters' dowry was seven years of labour finally realised that his nephew was not settling for that arrangement anymore. This man who had been dictating the pace till now was finally put into the defensive: he then asked for terms and agreed to give him his back pay with every speckled or spotted sheep, every dark-coloured lamb and every spotted or speckled goat in the flock. Jacob could do this because he had made great impact on the business of his uncle and father in law. Jacob was skilled in raising the flock and was therefore left in charge though Laban had sons. As a young worker seek skill and relevance and with time your employers will pay you enough to worth your time.

Stay away from jobs or careers where you are reminded all the time that your contribution is irrelevant and that you can be replaced easily when you leave. You will never be paid well under such a circumstance and your frustrations will prevent you from excelling at that job or career. Remember you reap what you sow: any job that you are not giving your best and are getting paid above your input, you will not be able to do something meaningful with the pay they give you. Always work harder than you are paid and you will be promoted sooner than later to occupy the next higher position to get a salary or benefit to merit the extra effort you are putting into the work. Remember that you are similar in qualification and experience with a lot of people and the things which will make you stand out are the extra things you do at work that others are reluctant to do because it is too hard or because it is not part of their job description or they feel it's beneath them. The two things which give fast rise in any career are competence and interpersonal skills: they are not always in this order sometime interpersonal skills are even ranked even higher than competence.

You have planted much, but harvested little. You eat, but never have enough. You drink, but never have your fill. You put on clothes, but are not warm. You earn wages, only to put them in a purse with holes in it (Haggai 1:6)."

To avoid wasting your income keep track of it using the ten percent you give us tithes. I started this habit ten years ago and after targeting higher ten percent of my income to give for the work of God (tithe) every New Year, I saw my income increase quicker than any pay rise because of inflation. Income or wages are seeds that are given to you to build your life. They are not amounts you depend on hoping it will increase by the grace of your government or employer. You need to sow income into ventures which will also yield income to add to the salary or wage you receive. The only income you can be sure of is the income you control and not the one your employer pays you. Take steps early to invest in things which will bring you additional income so you can take your time to gain skill and experience before you move from job to job solely on the basis of not receiving adequate income.

Assets

Many under thirties are not fully aware of all that the lord has entrusted to them. Their preoccupation is mostly with the more costly things they own and because they don't fully know their net worth by checking periodically they wake up one day and realise their liabilities have surpassed their assets. Others also mistakenly see things which cost them money to maintain and do not hold their value over time as assets and keep buying them. Overtime their lives become littered with things which do not bring income and are soon out of fashion or worn out. But every great person in the Bible has his entire assets enumerated even to the slaves or employee they had. Let us consider two of such reviews of the assets of a tribe and the assets of the greatest man in the east. Observe how the knowledge of these assets inform the conversation about them. Again observe how their assets affected their walk with their maker.

"*Let Reuben live and not die, nor[a] his people be few* (Deuteronomy 33:6)."

The bible says like arrows in the hands of a warrior so are children to their parents because they can be sent ahead of them into the future to accomplish things they, the parent could not do. But Reuben the first born son of Jacob was cursed by his father for taking his young wife and years later when Moses counted Rueben's descendants realised the curse was still working. The descendants of Reuben were dwindling in terms of fighting men who were the strength of the tribe. Far younger tribes were much bigger in terms of fighting men and were therefore in line to receive more land than the eldest tribe of Rueben.

Moses was saddened by this development and prayed to God to overturn this curse of Jacob. Moses only became aware of this after an exercise to assess the strength of each tribe. There are many going round with a false sense of importance because they have borrowed to buy expensive things. Most of these people forget that their liabilities are far more than the things they have bought and are therefore effectively worse off than they started.

The story of a colleague of mine at my first job, who was also a traditional ruler illustrates the importance of keeping track of net worth clearly. When he died and family member gathered to share his estate they were confronted with so many demands for repayment of borrowed funds. When the family announced for all the creditors to gather the number was so huge it could have been mistaken for a festival. The family quickly closed the gathering with an excuse after realising the man's debts far exceeded the properties he had left behind. It became apparent that this precarious situation and its impending shame might have contributed to his untimely death.

In the land of Uz there lived a man whose name was Job. This man was blameless and upright; he feared God and shunned evil. He had seven sons and three daughters, and he owned seven thousand sheep, three thousand camels, five hundred yoke of oxen and five hundred donkeys, and had a large number of servants. He was the greatest man among all the people of the East (Job 1:1-3).

Above is Job's net worth: the assessment of all that he owned and all who worked for him for life, even to the point of how he ranked amongst the great men of the east at the time. This background puts the succeeding story in its proper context. It clearly tells us that the owner of multiple businesses with grown children can still be upright before God. It brings to the fore the possibility of becoming wealthy without compromising our faith. One of the reasons formerly colonised countries are still under developed is the fact that these nations' citizens had no idea of how their country was doing in terms of statistics on their economy for hundreds of years. When their colonial masters were around they had no access to such data until about six decades ago when they took over the reins that they started compiling and reviewing GDP data from time to time for themselves.

About ten years ago I caught this revelation and started reviewing my net worth every month and made a table to compare them from year to year to see if I am increasing or decreasing. This practice helps me know much of my income is going into loans, car repairs, to support family and into investments. Any time I find myself not following steps which support the goals I have set for my life I adjusted it to suit the goals. There are many people blaming the devil for stealing their money because they do not know what they do with it. Please develop the habit of writing down your assets and liabilities at least once every month and you will realise which areas of your life are contributing to the waste of your income. Again your net assets review will show you where your heart really is: because you will see what you spend most of your money on. It will also give you ideas of what else to do to improve your net worth before the next review.

Because Job was a worthy God fearing man his impact on his community was great. No wonder the Lord was please to use him as a reference point to His adversary the devil. Learn to count your blessing and name them one by one and the provider of all things will add to them. How do you know you have lost one sheep out of a hundred unless you keep record? And how can you keep record of what you are in charge of unless you are a good shepherd? Dear reader, never lose sight of what God has entrusted into your care.

Counting the cost

"Suppose one of you wants to build a tower. Won't you first sit down and estimate the cost to see if you have enough money to complete it? For if you lay the foundation and are not able to finish it, everyone who sees it will ridicule you, saying, 'This person began to build and wasn't able to finish.' "Or suppose a king is about to go to war against another king. Won't he first sit down and consider whether he is able with ten thousand men to oppose the one coming

against him with twenty thousand? If he is not able, he will send a delegation while the other is still a long way off and will ask for terms of peace (Luke 14:28 – 32).

A man or woman of means or worth if he wants to be able to increase it keep it, he or she will have to be able to see into the future a plan for it. As a youth you should be able to see your future through prayer and planning of battles and its spoils which lay ahead. See the victories and potential obstacle ahead and pray into them before those events are suddenly upon you. The good book says that the wise man sees trouble ahead and avoids it; but the fool walk right into it. May it never be your portion in Jesus name! After learning how to assess your network the gaps will become apparent to you. You will then need to come out with a plan to improve upon your life. The next chapter will teach us habits to adopt to set us towards many worthwhile goals.

GOLD NUGGETS

Knowing how to access my net worth

1) Know your debt taken for investments and have a plan to reduce it before it overwhelms you
2) Know how to access your income and the strategies to improve income far above inflation.
3) Knowing how to assess your assets periodically and its review to ensure net improvement year upon year.
4) Learn how to project into the future to estimate occurrences for good or evil and take steps to avert them before they become reality.

HABIT 3: THE ART OF SETTING SMART GOALS

Is there not a cause

David listened to the same narrative of what kind of reward will be given the slayer of Goliath like the other soldiers had heard for forty days. But no one saw the motivation of becoming a prince and the added advantage of never paying tax good enough to even offer to fight the philistine champion. Here was an opportunity to be a royal and a free ticked to riches presented to soldiers who were already sworn to die and no one took it for more than a month. David stepped there one afternoon and soon understood what the deal meant for himself and his entire family.

This under thirty had this perspective in life because he knew he has been anointed as a king in waiting. He had a purpose beyond just fighting Goliath: he saw it as a step closer to becoming what the lord has anointed him to be. His senior brothers saw what the opportunity could do for David after they have been rejected by God and scolded him for being proud. To them, David had that posturing because of the anointing: that he thinks he is special because God has set him apart for the special assignment of leading Israel someday.

Now the Israelites had been saying, "Do you see how this man keeps coming out? He comes out to defy Israel. The king will give great wealth to the man who kills him. He will also give him his daughter in marriage and will exempt his family from taxes in Israel." David asked the men standing near him, "What will be done for the man who kills this Philistine and removes this disgrace from

Israel? Who is this uncircumcised Philistine that he should defy the armies of the living God?" (1 Samuel 17:25-26).

Events after David killed Goliath indeed set him on the part to the throne to the point that even the heir of King Saul who was also a fine specimen for kingship even ceded it to him without a fight. What happened? When David expressed interest in fighting Goliath it was reported to the King and the Bible says after talking to Saul and assuring him that he is able to kill the philistine champion, Jonathan the heir apparent's soul was knit to his and he loved him more than a woman's love for a man. This act of offering to kill Goliath set things in motion for David and eventually got him the throne. For the youth without a plan every difficulty is an obstacle that must be avoided. Many have scaled their springboards to fame and relevance into obscurity because they had no way to consider how the obstacle could help propel them closer to their goals in life.

Have life goals

As it is widely declared: an unexamined life is not worth living. A life without goals is like a car that is moving without destination or defined course for the driver to take. Such a car will be avoided by all right thinking beings because any place can suddenly become the road it uses as its journeys nowhere. A life without goals is a life that is unexamined because there are no benchmarks to compare things with.

Goals are the things you work towards in life: goals could be life long, medium term and short term. Goals could be spiritual, emotional or physical. You can set spiritual goals. Paul said: that I might know him and the power of his resurrection and the fellowship of his suffering. After he achieved most of his spiritual goals he said: I have run the race, I have finished my course and what is left for me is a crown of righteousness. You cannot finished a course until you are fully aware of it. Paul had a spiritual vision to reach all of the gentiles of his era and he fulfilled it.

Jesus was fully aware of why he came to this world so he was able to achieve his mission in three short years: a mission that has taken us more than two millennia to wrap up. When Jesus started His ministry he went to a synagogue and read His goals to the congregation from the book of Isaiah chapter 61 versus 1. The spirit of the lord is upon me and He has anointed me to preach the gospel to the poor, bring hope to the hopeless, to declare the year of jubilee. No one in this word has achieved anything meaningful without written down goals. Put down some lifelong goals, career goals, relationship goals and above all some goals in the service of your maker. And grace will be made available to help bring them to pass.

Have medium term goals

Jacob used six years to become rich after working for fourteen years with only love on his mind. He became rich because he had a plan to recover all the wages he had lost over the fourteen years. The reality of life without a medium term goal dawn on him when he saw himself penniless with two wives who were busily competing for his attention by bringing forth children. He saw the cost of living increasing beyond his ability to cope with each passing year. He saw himself broke twenty years to come without his own herds still dependant on his father in-law. This realisation caused him to revaluate his life for the past fourteen years. The results of his evaluation woke him from his love stupor: he then said to the man who gave him his love Rachel, that you have cheated me all this years though I have made you rich. Rachel was no longer adequate compensation for his fourteen years' service after he saw the future.

For it was little which thou hadst before I came, and it is now increased unto a multitude; and the Lord hath blessed thee since my coming: and now when shall I provide for mine own house also? And he said, What shall I give thee? And Jacob said, Thou shalt not give me any thing: if thou wilt do this thing for me, I will again feed and keep thy flock. I will pass through all thy flock to day, removing from thence all the speckled and spotted cattle, and all the brown cattle among the sheep, and the spotted and speckled among the goats: and of such shall be my hire (Genesis 30:30-32).

After seeing a medium term plan to become his own man in his man's eye he suddenly saw himself as a business partner instead of an employee. He then demanded back pay in the form of shares in the business.

His medium term goals of becoming financially free gave him a fighting spirit and ingenious ideas. It is your goals which will create the resources you need to achieve them. Your vision will make you and not you who will make the vision. Plan before you turn thirty to own a share of a growing business or assets and you will be setting yourself up for life.

Have spiritual goals

Here is a trustworthy saying: Whoever aspires to be an overseer desires a noble task (1Timothy3:1).

Please develop spiritual goals early in life: investigate your passions, talents and gifts and identify the call of God upon your life early. Know your calling early because there will be a lot to learn in your ministry. Start early and learn from your mistakes at a far younger age where you are teachable and have the hunger to succeed. There is a reason most of the ministers who started ministry before the age of thirty made a worldwide impact. Most worthwhile goals in life need time to mature: especially visions which require the buy in of people. Please use your passion to pioneer and grow a spiritual vision before it is all spent in getting a spouse.

Have relationship goals

*One who has unreliable friends soon comes to ruin, but there is a friend who sticks closer than a brother (*Proverbs 18:24*).*

As a young person some of the most important people in your life will be your friends. Young people are so committed to friends that they can easily abandoned all that the parents have thought them and follow what pleases their friends. To be an excellent youth you need to have goals for the kind of friends you will want to keep for the rest of your lives. In life the number of your true friends will reduce as you grow till you are left with few friends and many acquaintances. Since you are the sum of the five closest people to you, make sure you choose them wisely to fit your life goals. Choose friends who challenge you to give off your best in life. Friends you can draw inspiration from when things are difficult. Friends who can correct you when you go wrong. Friends who are not envious of your progress in life because they are progressive themselves. Good friends can be more reliable than blood brothers in times of adversity so choose them wisely before age thirty.No one is truly a self-made man: everyone is helped on his or her way to greatness. The next chapter will show you how to build the right relationships for a life of excellence.

GOLD NUGGETS

The art of setting goals

1) Have a life changing reason for everything you do and you will find the strength to surmount every challenge life throws at you.
2) Have goals for every worthwhile endeavour in your life because you will not make your goals but your goals will most likely make you.
3) Your goals should include your spiritual life: aim to grow from grace to grace.
4) Have goals for your relationships: most of the things God will give you in life will be through people so invest in your relationship to reflect your goals.

HABIT 4: NETWORKING

David's network of safety

David came to prominence early in life, he is an example of someone who showed signs of excellence before his twenties. This early rise of David ensured that he had time to learn from his mistakes and to build worthwhile networks or alliances. David's ability to form networks was so good that he even had friends amongst the enemies of Israel.

Jonathan said to David, "Go in peace, for we have sworn friendship with each other in the name of the Lord, saying, 'The Lord is witness between you and me, and between your descendants and my descendants forever.'" Then David left, and Jonathan went back to the town (1 Samuel 20:42).

David's was seen as a contender for the throne yet the very person he was going to oust was in his network and even helped him escape death from his own father. Jonathan was a great warrior and could have stood successfully against David to defend his throne but did not because he was close to David enough to know that the Lord had anointed him to sit on that throne and so deserved it more than him.

*So he left them with the king of Moab, and they stayed with him as long as David was in the stronghold (*1 Samuel 22:4*).*

David a young teenager who was left with few sheep in the wilderness by his father without companions used the opportunities he found in King Saul's palace and in the army to build connections with the kings of Moab and Gath, nations which were constantly at war with Israel. These alliances were lifesaving when King Saul was after his life. These networks helped David sneak in and out of Israel undetected. David could have continued with the lone ranger persona he endured as a shepherd but he chose to get allies to help in things which affected his nation and gain many allies as a result.

Professional network

So David and his men, about six hundred in number, left Keilah and kept moving from place to place. When Saul was told that David had escaped from Keilah, he did not go there (1 Samuel 23:13).

David raised as a shepherd saw an opportunity to escape the loneliness and took it to kill Goliath. That singular act moved him into prominence and eradicated poverty form his family. The same opportunity others saw and thought of all that could go wrong if they stepped forward. David built such strong rapport with his fellow soldiers that many found more safety with him compared to the national army. David's network of friends helped protect him and his family as he moved around like a fugitive.

David's destiny would have been cut short but for the protection his network of friends provided. There is a reason every government is largely family and friends. For you can only work with people you trust or people the people you trust recommend to you. Hence, learn to remember faces and names. And do not stay for a considerable length of time at any place without leaving an acquaintance behind. David went on errands to Gath and struck an important acquaintance which saved his life in the later years when he got in trouble with his master Saul. Please stop saying you have no one because everyone needs someone.

That day David fled from Saul and went to Achish king of Gath (1 Samuel 21:10).

Having a network of people is so important that democracy and winning elections depend on it. No matter the ideas you have you need people in your network to sell you before you will appeal to the masses. Have a network of course mates, schoolmates, year mates, professional body mates etc. The people in this network will be walking and breathing advertising boards for you in your career, when you need character reference and in building wealth. There are jobs you can only get because you belong to a particular network. Your network will be your platform to test ideas and pitch business that you hope to roll out to the masses if you use it well. Please don't waste your networks on social media on arguments and pranks but use it as a spring board to soar higher in the things which matter in your life. You cannot do anything really impactful in life unless you are connected to a great network of friends. Someone said and I agree that you need a maximum of three people to get in touch with anyone no matter their status in this world.

You need to know someone, who knows someone and you will find yourself in the presence of this person or you will find yourself interacting with the person on social media, telephone or through emails. Networks are a catalyst which can put you far ahead of your peers. David was anointed and extremely talented but endured loneliness in the wilderness because he knew no one. But to last at the height of his power he needed a network of highly intelligent as well as brave men and women. You may go fast alone but certainly not very far and not for very long.

Maintaining a Network

The Bible teaches on how to keep friends: be friendly if you want to keep friends it admonishes. The same rule applies in keeping networks working together for your good. Each network and what you can provide to remain relevant professional.

Oxford University Professor Robin Dunbar has conducted a study of social groupings throughout the centuries, from neolithic villages to modern office environments. His findings, based on his theory 'Dunbar's number', developed in the 1990s, asserts that size of the part of the brain used for conscious thought and language, the neocortex, limits us to managing 150 friends, no matter how sociable we are[20].

As has been demonstrated above your brain can keep up with the management of friends up to about 150.But you do not need more than this number of friends to make great networks. In every group and I am sure you have observed that in school and on the various social media platforms: there are the alphas or the dominant members of each group and their 'say so' carries the day in the group. To keep great networks you need to strife to be the dominant character or with the dominant characters of the group. Once your relationship with the few dominant characters is good the rest of the group will assume you are good with them. You can therefore have good friends numbering thirty and be a major mover or shaker in the society so long as these friends are part of a wider network of friends.

This wisdom of knowing when size is more important and when it is not is summed up in an African proverb which literally translated means: *you send a wise son on an errand and not the son who can walk to far places.* Make quality friends who will contribute positively to your life and not convenient ones whose only interest will be what they can get from you.

After learning how to make the right kind of friends their positive influence will help you imbibe habits which will propel you to the top of whatever endeavour you are involved in. What do you do when the income from your labour start coming in and you are torn between immediate or future gratification. The next chapter talks about how to handle income for a prosperous life.

GOLD NUGGETS

Networking

1) Build a network of safety which will bear you up in prayers or physically come to your aid when in trouble.
2) Build a professional network for your learning and recommendation when positions come up in your industry or ministry.
3) To maintain a network you need to identify the dominant personalities in the group because every group has 'alphas' controlling the activities of the group.
4) A man who needs a network to work for him must himself be helpful in the networks he belongs to.

HABIT 5: KNOWING INVESTMENTS AND WEALTH BUILDING

Wealth

Cast your bread upon the waters, For you will find it after many days. Give a serving to seven, and also to eight, For you do not know what evil will be on the earth. If the clouds are full of rain, They empty themselves upon the earth; And if a tree falls to the south or the north, In the place where the tree falls, there it shall lie. He who observes the wind will not sow, And he who regards the clouds will not reap

(Ecc 11:1-4, NKJV)[21].

The above scripture sums up the strategies of wealth creation. Please start the journey of wealth creation before age thirty. Learn to build wealth even before marriage because status in life affects our decision of who we choose to marry or who we accept to marry. Let your spouse meet you financially sound or with a financially sound strategy. Do not be in a position where most of your major lives decisions are based on who or what will deliver you out of poverty.

Why do we need to be wealthy early? What is wealth? And what makes wealth so important in the life of an individual? Wealth is the abundance of valuable possessions or money. Wealth is important because it provides influence, safety and sustains life. As explained in the scripture above wealth comes about when we save, invest, take calculated risk and protect the valuable things in our lives with security and insurance. Most of the very rich people in the world were wealthy before they were thirty years. Remember you will 'find your bread after many days': time is your greatest ally when building sustainable wealth. The earlier you start the easier it will be for you to build great wealth.

Savings

No matter what you earn in wages, salary or investment yield, you need to develop the discipline of living below your means. Always spend less than you earn. Living without savings is like saying your entire life's expenses will always be equivalent to your income. An impossibility of the highest order. Without savings you cannot take advantage of reduced to clear goods or property. Without savings you will always buy things on high purchase: which is usually much more expensive than buying them with ready cash. Without savings it will not be possible to buy property without securing loans with interest. Save or you will be forced to commit a greater part of your income to servicing loans on everything you purchase. In a high inflation and currency depreciation economy like most developing countries savings are for a short time, usually less than three months for purchasing something valuable.

Compound interest

Compound interest is a situation where the principal you invested yields interest and the interest also yields interest. When money is invested consistently in a safe instrument which does not lose value the principal amount yields interest which when rolled over leads to the interest also becoming another principal to also yield interest therefore compounding. Compound interest yield best when you start early and are consistent with your investment with little or no withdrawals. Starting consistent investment in your twenties instead of thirties could make the difference from you having a yield of a million instead of few hundred thousand. Read about investments and start putting your windfalls into a good investment portfolio right away.

Money market

Learn about the money market and how interest rate and inflation affects worth creation early. Study the various product offered by investment and asset management companies. Select what is suitable to your investment yield appetite and learn to assess the risk it comes with. Generally high yielding investment vehicles are often more risky and vice versa. Starting early will help you to make the necessary changes to your portfolio in good time before your losses become colossal in later years.

 Learn to let your money work for you whilst you sleep. Make interest rate a friend instead of an enemy: for interest rate together with inflation will gradually steal your wealth over time if not checked. Examples of money market products are the balance funds, mutual funds, government bills, unit funds, and various bank deposits. It is generally advised that you start with less risky instruments and move to more sophisticated ones as you gain more knowledge. Invest for cash flow or in appreciating assets.

Build businesses

Business is the activity of making one's living or making money by producing or buying and selling goods or services.[22] Business is simply providing solutions to lives challenges for a fee. You are in good business when customers see your products or services as more rewarding than the prices you are charging. The most profitable businesses now, especially those in the technology sector were founded by people in their twenties. From late teens to the twenties you might probably still have some support from your parents and can therefore be more adventurous in starting businesses.

Having a fall-back position of parental support without children and wife to worry about can be the difference between your business surviving or otherwise. Most people who are wealthy in this world are people doing one business or the other. Even investors invest in businesses to become wealthy. Your business can stem from needs you identify in your surroundings, or from the skills acquired in training for careers or from harnessing your talent. Most wealthy nations became worthy because from their founding they have had companies selling goods and services on a very large scale.

Build multiple streams of income

It is a very dangerous thing to depend on one source of income. This way of living is a product of the industrial era where people worked for one company till they retired on a fat pension. A pay check is the value of your service for a period: could be per hour, weekly or monthly. What it is saying is that your time is worth this match. There are people whose hourly income values are equivalent to someone's monthly pay. This does not mean that their job is several times more important than the person earning far less but that the richer person is earning small amounts from several sources at the same time whiles the poorer earner is on just an income.

Adam was assigned to a garden with trees, flowers, animal, and rivers to benefit from and not to earn a living from a single tree no matter how big. There is no single worthy person in the Bible who had one source of income: consider Job, Abraham, Isaac and this will become even clearer. Start from one source, parents, gifts, job then through investments and find economically viable solutions to problems and with the income build other streams over the years till you are financially secure.

Give a serving to seven, and also to eight, For you do not know what evil will be on the earth. (Ecclesiastes 11:2, NKJV).[23]

Insurance

Usually insurance is seen as the thing you do because you do not want the police to arrest you but that is far from the reality. Insurance is the assurance against any eventuality. It helps you recover property that you have used years to acquire after a disaster. Without insurance many people will move from years of wealth to poverty suddenly, if their source of income was destroyed. Insurance will prevent you from struggling over a car with an armed robber because you know the car is not being lost because you can recover most of the cost from your insurer. People instead of running for dear life after calling the fire service instead stay to douse the fire themselves because they cannot bear to see their life investment go up in smoke and end up dying.

But if the house and its contents are insured you will be more incline to save your life because you know you can recover most of what is destroyed with your claim. Insurance takes the burden of 'what if this happens' and assures you that, so long us the cause is accidental or natural you are covered. Take insurance to avoid losing everything you have worked for in a disaster.

GOLD NUGGETS

Knowing investment and worth building

1) Learn to save for assets acquisition and for emergency expenses to avoid incurring debt in such situations.
2) Start studying investment early and decide an investment strategy to reflect your lifelong goals.
3) Use insurance to secure property against theft, fire and other acts of nature. This will prevent you from starting afresh anytime there is a disaster and give you the time to build wealth.
4) Learn to increase your streams of income till they can sustain you without a full time work.

HABIT 6: LEVERAGE

Introduction

Before we get into all the technicalities of leverage and all the forms it takes in the world of business, engineering and finance let us explain it simply. Leverage is simply finding help where you lack the strength, time or number to do more than you would have if you did with your effort alone. To a young lady leverage is getting that wig or high heel to enhance her beauty to attract a suitable partner. Leverage to a young preacher with a congregations of forty is social media platforms where he can reach thousands with just one messages for years to come. Leverage simply put is a system which helps multiply efforts. Such is the power of leverage to quickly transform our lives for the very best in the shortest of time that every young person needs to learn to use it quickly.

Leverage

According to Business Dictionary 2018, leverage is the ability to influence a system, or an environment, in a way that multiplies the outcome of one's efforts without a corresponding increase in the consumption of resources. In other words, leverage is the advantageous condition of having a relatively small amount of cost yield a relatively high level of returns[24].

Leverage is simply a system which multiplies effort: it helps magnify the effort you put in work to get the desired outcome. Technology is leverage in the communication of vision or in the publicising of products to family and friends. With technology like social media a message that you would have otherwise had to send one after the other to several people can be made available to thousands of people at the push of a button. The media on the other hand can be used to reach millions after one program has been recorded. There are recorded programs which have been shown to millions whilst the actors were engaged in other activities because of the leverage of recorded broadcast. Learn to use technology to reach more people at a cheaper cost with your vision or with the products you are marketing.

Other people's talents in a group can be leverage to help us achieve things which would have taken us years to do all by ourselves. That is why choosing a good team helps in achieving wonderful things as a ministry or company. Behind every great company or ministry is an even greater team. Your own talent will not take you far; you can only make a worldwide impact when you leverage the talents and efforts of many in a team towards a definite purpose. Every great leader is a man or woman who has learnt to harness an environment or leverage a system to achieve far more than they could have on their own. According to Plato even the world can be lifted using the right lever: that is how powerful leverages are. Do not neglect using that power in your life.

Financial Leverage

Leverage is any technique involving the use of borrowed funds in the purchase of an asset, with the expectation that the after tax income from the asset and asset price appreciation will exceed the borrowing cost.[2] Unlike borrowing for consumption which leads to poverty and enslavement, leverage when done right enables you to increase income at an incremental rate. It is like taking a no interest loan at your work place to invest in the short term money markets: where the interest gain is more than the loan deductions. In this way you gain without actually having to spend years trying to accumulate the funds. Additionally you get the opportunity to benefit 100% from something that you will pay for over a period of months or even years. Leveraging should not be used for businesses where the principal amount and interest cannot be guaranteed or the money will be lost and it will become like any other debt that you have incurred and have nothing to show for it. Leverage other people's talents and contacts to build wealth for your generation and the next.

GOLD NUGGETS

1) Learn to use leverage to build wealth quicker than using proceeds from savings for investment every time.
2) Leverage is using a system to help you do more than you could have done by yourself.
3) Leverage technology to get your vision or products to the masses at less cost and effort.
4) Learn to tap other people's talents in a group or team to achieve far more than you would have if you had relied on your own talents alone.

HABIT 7: THE USE OF MY TALENT

Identifying your talent

According to Merriam-Webster talent[25] *is a special often athletic, creative, or artistic aptitude; general intelligence or mental power: ability; the natural endowments of a person.* A talent is therefore innate or genetic. You are born with it and its most often noticed by your friends, siblings or parents early in life. Talents can therefore be skills you possess in sports, athletic or the arts. Talents can also be mental: in the form intelligence or ability to memorise. Like most things natural talent is a raw gem which needs to be polished through study and practice for it to shine. Talents are skills or abilities which comes to us naturally but needs nurturing to grab the attention of the world.

The uniqueness of most talents makes them extremely appealing to the average person. This attribute of talents make them great money earners in the field of sports and entertainment. Any footballers who is at the top of his or her game started training at most in their teens or as children. There are some talents especially, in music or sports which if training does not start with children there will be no chance of making it to the top because your body would have become too set for it to be moulded with training for a world class performance. If you have a talent set for yourself goals and work at reaching the top with diligence and advance information on techniques to get better.

People affirming your talent by recommendation

As you grow up from childhood people will attest to your extra skill at one thing or the other. They will make comments about your seeming obsession with one activity or the other. This will be mostly amongst your friends and family. As you work at your talent it will be recognised by school or community and people you encounter on a regular basis. Then when an activity is mentioned and you are talented in the area people will begin to nominate you for that role. Everyone on any stage of life performing any talented activity you can think of started because someone recognised his or her talent and recommended him for that role. You will stop your talent from developing if you get in the habit of not preparing for roles assigned to you or declining to act when appointed by others. So if you do not know your talent: the clue is that when people are needed for certain activities you are the first on peoples' mind and they will mention you to be most suited for the role. This is a clear testimony that people have recognised that talent in your life and have agreed that you are better at that activity than others.

Burying talent

The Parable of the Talents

"For the kingdom of heaven is like a man traveling to a far country, who called his own servants and delivered his goods to them. And to one he gave five talents, to another two, and to another one, to each according to his own ability; and immediately he went on a journey. Then he who had received the five talents went and traded with them, and made another five talents. And likewise he who had received two gained two more also. But he who had received one went and dug in the ground, and hid his lord's money.

After a long time the lord of those servants came and settled accounts with them. "So he who had received five talents came and brought five other talents, saying, 'Lord, you delivered to me five talents; look, I have gained five more talents besides them.' His lord said to him, 'Well done, good and faithful servant; you were faithful over a few things, I will make you ruler over many things. Enter into the joy of your lord.' He also who had received two talents came and said, *'Lord, you delivered to me two talents; look, I have gained two more talents besides them.'* His lord said to him, *'Well done, good and faithful servant; you have been faithful over a few things, I will make you ruler over many things. Enter into the joy of your lord.'*

"Then he who had received the one talent came and said, *'Lord, I knew you to be a hard man, reaping where you have not sown, and gathering where you have not scattered seed. And I was afraid, and went and hid your talent in the ground. Look, there you have what is yours.'* "But his lord answered and said to him, *'You wicked and lazy servant, you knew that I reap where I have not sown, and gather where I have not scattered seed. So you ought to have deposited my money with the bankers, and at my coming I would have received back my own with interest. So take the talent from him, and give it to him who has ten talents. 'For to everyone who has, more will be given, and he will have abundance; but from him who does not have, even what he has will be taken away. And cast the unprofitable servant into the outer darkness. There will be weeping and gnashing of teeth.'* (Matthew 25:14-30, NKJV).[25]

To get the full import of the seriousness of burying talent the full scripture above has been quoted. The story above clearly shows that talents are not the same neither are they at the same level for everyone. It also shows that when talents is properly deployed it brings multiplication of the talent. Again we learned that when talents is multiplied in its deployment, it brings ruler ship or influence. But when talent is buried as a result of the fear of the outcome of deploying it, the result is deprivation and gnashing of teeth. There are many talented footballers who through coaching and training have ended up playing on the world stage and through their incomes completely eradicated poverty from their nuclear families. Identify your talent early and work at it till it puts you on the world stage.

There are many talented people who are still in the shadows or left in one desolate corner of the world because they had no one to market their abilities. There are many stories of better footballers ending up broke whilst their less talented team mate end up playing on the world stage because of a good agent who exposed or marketed them to the right people. You are talented yes, but that is not enough you need to learn to take steps to market that ability to the rest of the world sooner than later if you want to go places. The next chapter deals with the issues of selling or marketing.

GOLD NUGGETS

The use of my talent

1) Talents are innate: thus things you are born with. Therefore talents are not only what you do but also what you are.
2) Genuine talents will be seen by others apart from yourself so do not be quick to discount it when people point you to it.
3) Talent as it grows with practice will be recommended by friends and relatives to other people.
4) It takes much more effort to bury a talent than to come out with it for the world to benefit.
5) You are born with raw talent and needs polishing to make it shine to the rest of the world.

HABIT 8: THE ART OF MARKETING OR SELLING

Helping parents sell

Marketing is the process or technique of promoting, selling, and distributing a product or service (Merriam-Webster, 2018)[26]. The art of selling, promoting or distribution of product or services is one of the most undeveloped of abilities in the lives of young people. Because most people avoid opportunities to learn how to sell as a child citing child labour and matters of safety. We often see the art of selling to help the home as a burden to avoid if we can. But this is an essential skill needed to push an agenda, sell a product or service. For the rest of your life you will be selling one thing or the other.

If you are not good at selling you will miss many job and business opportunities in life. Anyone with exceptional selling abilities will be able to walk in and out of great jobs seamlessly. There are many products with equivalent abilities and qualities: what is needed is someone to promote their sale or to market them. Marketing or selling highlights' the benefits of someone or something and tries to secure the buy in of the customer.

Power of Persuasion

One place where we learn marketing or selling is when we are called upon to raise funds for a course. People are always attached to their monies: a lot of skill is therefore needed to cause them to part with their monies for a good cause. It is even more difficult when they are giving their money for an intangible benefit like blessings. Sharpen your skills of persuasion by learning to convince people to commit to great courses.

Moses had to learn to sell himself in the palace of pharaoh daily because he was the son of a slave living like a prince in the palace. He had to convince himself daily he deserve to live with the masters of his countrymen and even had right to order some about sometimes. His skill of selling was therefore put to use when he had to convince all Israelites to leave the most powerful kingdom at the time to a land they had not seen by going through the barren desert. Talk about leaving your comfort zones by walking through the valley of the shadows of death to an imaginary place of comfort and you will not be far from right!

Preaching salvation to a crowd

Every sound preacher proclaims the year of jubilee to a perverse generation in the very act of sin. Sinning is the most enticing and addictive thing a person can get up to. That is why it takes a lot of power and careful marketing to convince people to leave it for a better life. Every great preacher is therefore a great marketer in deeds and appearance. Please learn to sell what God has laid on your heart or you will always be alone to pursue your vision. You will not have vision enablers to take you far in what you have envisioned to do if you cannot sell what God has placed on your heart to do, to others.

Then she came and told the man of God. And he said, "Go, sell the oil and pay your debt; and you and your sons live on the rest." (2 Kings 4:7)

This prophet's wife was still poor after a great miracle of a little oil becoming drums of oil. Her life was still the same till she started selling the excess oil which were sitting in her house. Only then was she able to pay of the family's life long debt and have excess to cash to look after herself and her family. You have prayed and God has intervened but your inability to sell is still keeping your business down. Sell, in fact start selling in your twenties or your vision will remain in your living room never to get out for the world to see.

Running for office

Politicians are simply sales men and women: selling visions and themselves to the electorate. Those who are good at selling usually win elections and not necessarily those who have their electorate at heart. That is why in any developed democracy there are mainly two dominant parties. Usually the parties which have the greatest appeal are those who have invested millions in advertisement to sell their ideals. In most places with developed democracies people vote by default because their preferred parties have been ingrained in them since childhood. To become a leader you need to develop the art of selling or your great ideas will never see the light of day.

Advertisement

I love a saying on a certain television station concerning advertisement: doing business without advertisement is like doing business in the dark, who will see you to patronise your product? David stood before Saul with just a short time to sell his talents and anointing. He had one chance to pitch the fact that he had strength to assume the office of the champion of Israel though a teenager and David still pulled it off. David had the unction upon him and was doing what no one in Israel was doing: killing lions and bears yet he was in charge of a few sheep with a father who did not count him amongst his worthy sons. David changed all that by advertising his talents before Saul. Every preacher is a salesman or woman, he or she is either selling himself or Christ.

Dear reader what are you selling? What skills, virtues or vision are you selling? Start selling or marketing early in life or your progress from the wilderness to the palace will delayed for a very long time.

As you market yourself and your gifts, you will attract many admirers and friends. You need to develop the ability to separate real friends from opportunist if your ministry, business or career will make any impact. The next chapter teaches how to discern genuine friends or partners for an excellent life.

GOLD NUGGETS

The art of marketing or selling

1) A city set on a hill in the spirit can be liken to a child of God who is marketing his Christian virtues to the rest of the world.
2) After the miracle of turning a small amount of oil into barrels of oil the prophet's widow was still in debt till she went out and started selling the oil then things turned around.
3) Some of the ways we demonstrate the art of selling: fund raising, preaching etc.
4) No matter how talented you are, you will not go far if you do not know how to sell your vision and demonstrate the grace of God upon your life to others.

HABIT 9: KNOWING HOW TO JUDGE CHARACTER

Character

As has been explained in earlier chapters, a man's character is simply the habits that he has formed over the years which are so prominent that they define him. *According to Merrian Webster, character is one of the attributes or features that make up and distinguish an individual. A synonym of character is disposition and disposition implies customary moods and attitudes toward the life around a person*[27].This clearly shows that character is a summary of the habits we have built over the years. This is why people are so different in many ways and yet very similar when they grow up exposed to similar circumstances. A man's behaviour or dispositions can therefore be predicted once his character is establish. In the same way a man's dominant disposition can be used to predict his character accurately.

Knowing the temperaments of People

Temperament is a characteristic or habitual inclination or mode of emotional response (Merrian Webster, 2018)[28.] Thus temperament is our habitual response to things in our environment. There are people I knew for years to be calm and quiet in secondary school but after university are now having a talkative and outgoing disposition. People can really change their dispositions under the right circumstances: that is why I am sure there is no one who is beyond character reformation. The Greco-Arabic concept of medicine uses four temperaments system: Sanguine, Phlegmatic, Choleric, and Melancholic Personality Types.

Knowing the dominant dispositions of people you encounter helps you choose friends carefully: being aware of their strengths and weaknesses. There are people who are naturally optimistic so when you tell them to do things and they say 'consider it done', you better supervise such people or you will be disappointed because it will not be done. Anyone who has made it in life knows how to select the right people for the right job. Knowing how to surround yourself with the right people is half the work done at succeeding in life. Jacob used his knowledge of his brother's temperament to take his birth right. Through this, Jacob became the father of Israel instead of Esau the eldest. Esau's lack of knowledge about temperament banished his descendants to a life of servitude to his brother's descendants.

Praying for the gift of discerning of spirits

There are times that you will encounter people who have over the years learnt to cloak their real character. There are people who have a chameleon disposition : they become anything the environment requires of them. People who are brought up under oppression or by very strict parents are very often skilled at pleasing people without it coming from the heart.

Slaves, obey your earthly masters with respect and fear, and with sincerity of heart, just as you would obey Christ (Ephesians 6:5).

Be careful of people who complain of oppression and abuse, because they tend to portray good behaviour without sincerity of heart. They are mostly world class pretenders who have perfected the art of appearing to please wicked bosses, guardians or partners. Pray for the spirit of discernment because the devil can appear as an angel of light how much more his human agents. Do much for people and expect very little from them and you will avoid many heart aches. Do not be swayed by a one sided story: no matter the tears shed telling it. No matter what, always hear from the other side before jumping to conclusion on a matter under contention. You will be surprised how many sides there are to a single story. Do not make enemies because you thought you were supporting the underdog.

Verifying things thoroughly before committing to them

Double check everything before you sign or agree to it. People are inherently selfish: they therefore make offers which they believe are to their advantage. The pressure is therefore on them to secure the sale or agreement and not on you the customer or client to agree. Take your time and peruse what is being offered, if possible seek for expert advice before you sign unto something that will ruin your life or career. People will pressurise you to settle for second best all the time: in relationships, career or property acquisition. You will be told to keep a potential suitor though all the signs are saying he or she is not good enough. You will be told to choose a less demanding job because no one in your family has even come close to what is being offered. You will be told to slow down and settle for something smaller because you are even lucky to get what is before you.

Always remember that you can either settle for average or stretch for excellence in all you do. This is a scenario you will be confronted with all the days of your young life. David could have chosen to be the armour bearer of the man who will fight Goliath instead he chose to fight himself without military training. Because if you the anointed is afraid of fighting for the best then what should the average person do. As a youth learn to fight for the best of everything, do not settle for less because life is not a rehearsal but the real deal. You will indeed come this way but once.

Saying No

You do not know someone enough till he or she has said no to you on a matter of importance. Learn to say no to people when necessary: giving in to ungrateful or wasteful members of your family and friends will only make them worse. Strive to be righteous and not merely good. A good person is seemingly loved by all but soon forgotten when his ability to help everyone is curtailed. The Bible says: woe to anyone who is loved by all because such a person will have to be a hypocrite to be able to satisfy peoples' competing interests. You need to develop the habit dear reader, of doing what is right before what is good or expedient. Learning to say no early will help you deal with erring children, subordinates and friends before they destroy your life. There are many prominent people whose reputation have been destroyed by their erring children because they did not say no to them when they were growing up. No one's love is genuine towards you till they are prepared to respect your 'no' to their request for one thing or the other. Remember you will never be considered principled till people have heard your no against things you consider to be wrong.

Knowing how to judge character will be an asset in choosing the people who will help you deploy your gifts in the service of God. To know the role of spiritual gifts in the life of excellent young men and women read the next chapter.

GOLD NUGGETS

Knowing how to judge character

1) You need to know the temperament of people and understand their strengths or weaknesses.
2) Pray for the gift of discernment of spirit because the devil likes to pose as an angel of light.
3) Check things thoroughly, including seeking for a second opinion before signing unto anything.
4) You never know anyone really well until he or she has said no to you: learn to say a firm no to those who breach your principals.

HABIT 10: THE USE OF MY SPIRITUAL GIFTS

Habit of praying in tongues

*For anyone who speaks in a tongue does not speak to people but to God. Indeed, no one understands them; they utter mysteries by the Spirit (*1 Corinthians 14:2*).*

One of the most dangerous aspect of life is when a spiritual man approaches life as though he is just a physical being trying to be spiritual.

All human beings are spirits with souls and live in a body. Bear with me if you thought this is some politically correct inspirational book which avoids anything spiritual like a plague. You, my dear reader are a spirit with a soul and a body. This is why you must never go through life thinking just sound advice will do. There is more to life than food and drink. Life is not only about nourishing your body and making merry to the satisfaction of your soul. The devil is battling for your mind because that is where all wars are waged for your eternal destiny. You eat everyday so you will be strong: you eat a balanced diet so you can grow healthily and function properly. In the same way feed your spirit because the spirit needs to grow from strength to strength. Eat the sincere milk and meat of the word for nourishment and healthy spiritual growth.

Pray in tongues daily for the growth of your spirit and you will be ushered into the all-powerful realm of spiritual men and women. The spiritual realm is where decisions are taken before they happen on earth. Having access to this realm enables you to foresee events and gives you the opportunity to intervene in the lives of God's people. As a youth, develop the habit of praying in tongues consistently to help grow your spiritual senses: uncovering the gifts and talents of God at your disposal.

Anyone who speaks in a tongue edifies themselves, but the one who prophesies edifies the church (1 Corinthians 14:4).

As you go through life you will see and hear lewd things and may have disagreements with relatives, friends etc. which may lead to arguments or even fights. These carnal activities that we fall in from time to time weakens us in the spirit: we therefore need to be edified by speaking in tongues from time to time. This is why a church which does not believe in tongues harbours many carnal church members and teach part of the truth instead of the whole truth of the scriptures. For it when the spirit of God has come upon us that we are lead to all through.

Fire in My Palm

I got born again at the age of fifteen and the Holy Spirit baptised me the same year. I would wait till everyone had left home and would pray in tongues constantly for hours. No one told me that I was empowering my spirit and needed to put the power to some spiritual use. I was so enthralled by the intoxication of the spirit that I just prayed for praying sake. Then one day at the height of prayer I felt my palm burning. Thinking of how to quench this invisible fire, I rushed to the kitchen and dipped my hands in water. In my ignorance I stopped praying fearing there will be a recurrence. This abrupt end to my spiritual 'marathon' activities affected me greatly through the years because my spiritual abilities went down gradually till they were almost none existent. I understand better now and will never quench the spirit ever again.

Use of Prophecy

In ancient times and even in the not so distant past young people from prominent families consulted oracles of all sorts to know the future and the path that have been set for them in life. The fore knowledge they gained from these encounters with the priest then served as a guide to them as they went through life. To excel in this competitive life you need to have some guidance as to where your strength is and where there could be pitfalls. The gift of prophecy encompasses the gift of speaking God's mind in church or speaking to God's people in a meeting. It also includes giving prophecy in tongues and then interpreting the tongues to edify the church or group of believers. Some believers speak in prophetic tongues without interpretation but that does not edify anyone until they are able to interpret. Prophecy when well-developed can produced an entire message to guide you in your Christian life.

Follow the way of love and eagerly desire gifts of the Spirit, especially prophecy. But the one who prophesies speaks to people for their strengthening, encouraging and comfort. Anyone who speaks in a tongue edifies themselves, but the one who prophesies edifies the church I would like every one of you to speak in tongues, but I would rather have you prophesy. The one who prophesies is greater than the one who speaks in tongues, unless someone interprets, so that the church may be edified (1 Corinthians 14:1, 3-5).

Dear reader, seek to excel in the gift of prophecy: many young men have had glorious ministries because of this single gift. This gift of the Word of knowledge or prophecy or instruction can bring directions which may change the cause of your life for ever. There are many young men and women who founded ministries or businesses because of a word of knowledge or instruction they received in a prayer meeting. Excel as a young Christian in this gift by exercising it according to faith and it will take you to great people and places.

Now, brothers and sisters, if I come to you and speak in tongues, what good will I be to you, unless I bring you some revelation or knowledge or prophecy or word of instruction? So it is with you. Since you are eager for gifts of the Spirit, try to excel in those that build up the church (1 Corinthians 14:-6, 12).

Develop understanding of how God speaks to you

As someone working with a spiritual God you need to learn to understand when he is speaking to you so you can follow his instructions. The Bible says that it is only those who follow the spirit of God who are sons of God indeed. But every child of God over the years will learn to distinctively separate God's voice from his or her own voice or thoughts. God's instructions always agree with the Bible; God's voice when followed makes us more spiritual; God's voice directs you to be more committed to his word and; God's voice when followed brings inner peace in spite of the turmoil that might be going on in your world because of the decision taken. Again God's voice will never encourage pride or lust but promote humility and self-control. Learn to hear him early and you will avoid many heartaches and headaches in life.

Exercising Spiritual Gifts

The gifts of the Holy Spirit are gifts that are given to the spirit of a born again Christian to help him or her meet both spiritual and physical needs of the Christian walk. The need for deliverance and healing led a lot of people before they became born again into the worship of evil spirits. Jesus after His ascension to heaven therefore gave gifts unto born again Christians to provide the solutions that as unbelievers they sought from demons. The gifts are given for various works in the church for believers to grow in faith and in the power of the Holy Spirit. As the Holy Spirit works these gifts in us, He teaches us to be loyal to Jesus, the king of kings. Spiritual gifts can only be desired:

you cannot forced them into your spirit because it is the Holy Spirit who considers your heart and gives to you as He wills. It is God's gift to men. Even the way the gifts are exercised are different and the way they are given to believers also differ somewhat. So work at your own gifts by listening to the promptings of the Spirit and the advice of senior ministers with similar gifts and calling.

Now about the gifts of the Spirit, brothers and sisters, I do not want you to be uninformed. You know that when you were pagans, somehow or other you were influenced and led astray to mute idols. Therefore I want you to know that no one who is speaking by the Spirit of God says, "Jesus be cursed," and no one can say, "Jesus is Lord," except by the Holy Spirit. There are different kinds of gifts, but the same Spirit distributes them. There are different kinds of service, but the same Lord. There are different kinds of working, but in all of them and in everyone it is the same God at work.

(1 Corinthians 12:1-6).

This chapter is showing you the fact that many young men and women are neither using their certificates or talents to impact society nor as the means for their livelihood but are using the gifts of the spirits to bring love and joy to the heart of many. You can avail yourself to the Spirit of God for this enablement. These spiritual gifts enable you to move seamlessly between the physical and the spiritual worlds as much as it is required for the benefit of a child of God. These gifts intervene in the physical world and imposes the will of God on the situation through a revelation, deliverance, healing and instruction. Use diverse gifts of the Holy Spirit to minister to believers in an atmosphere of miracles. Gifts of the Holy Spirit and the speaking of heavenly tongues show us the spiritual side of life and tell us what we can expect if we are more in the spirit than the flesh.

Now to each one the manifestation of the Spirit is given for the common good. To one there is given through the Spirit a message of wisdom, to another a message of knowledge by means of the same Spirit, to another faith by the same Spirit, to another gifts of healing by that one Spirit, to another miraculous powers, to another prophecy, to another distinguishing between spirits, to another speaking in different kinds of tongues, and to still another the interpretation of tongues. All these are the work of one and the same Spirit, and he distributes them to each one, just as he determines.

(1 Corinthians 12:7-11).

Learn from those who already operate in your gift

The great thing about learning is that you do not need to reinvent the wheel, whatever is happening now has been before for there is nothing new under the sun. Learn how the gifting's were used and avoid the mistakes of the past. Understand the steps that are needed to get into the spirit and the lifestyle changes required to operate under that grace. Remember spiritual gifts will take you to places but it is character which will keep the gifts working effectively. Use gifts according to your level of faith and do not be in a hurry to impress people. Be led throughout any ministration because the one in the driving seat is the Holy Spirit and not you.

Pray for more grace to impact with your gift because grace is access, grace is capacity and grace is endowment. Pray for the opportunity to display your gifts because the more you exercise them the more your faith grows. Pray for the ability to deploy the gifts with little human intervention: so as to allow the spirit of God to have His way in the service. Be diligent in studying, embarking on prayer and fasting to sharpen your understanding of your gifts because they can send you to places that formal education can never send you.

Having learnt to use the gifts of God in your life to minister to the needs of others you need to know what call of God is upon your life so you can walk with Him according to his perfect will. The next chapter addresses that so keep flipping the pages.

GOLD NUGGETS

The use of my spiritual gifts

1) Develop the habit of praying in tongues to boost spiritual strength against all that weighs you down in the flesh.
2) Learn to use the gift of prophecy to communicate God's loving desires for his children.
3) Exercise your mind and spirit to distinguish God's voice from you own voice so as to hear his clear instruction for your life.
4) Learn from those who operate in gifts similar to yours. This will help you master the use of your gifts early in life.

HABIT 11: KNOWING HOW TO LIVE ACCORDING TO GOD'S PURPOSE FOR MY LIFE

The Call

To excel in life you need to distinguish between a career or a vocation and answering the call of God. There are many people who are leading average, frustrated lives because they failed to yield to the call of God. Your greatness will be found in how you fulfil Gods call for your life.

But when God, who set me apart from my mother's womb and called me by his grace, was pleased to reveal his Son in me so that I might preach him among the Gentiles, my immediate response was not to consult any human being (Galatians 1:15-16).

Here, Paul the apostle was talking about when he received the call of God. Paul's experiences proved that he was set apart unto God from birth but only became aware of the call on the road to Damascus. The call of God is uncovered as you go through life. That is why the call can be seen by others before you become aware of it yourself sometimes. You carry your call from birth: you choose to activate it or leave it dormant for the rest of your life.

Paul also demonstrated in the scripture above that you need not be called to be zealous for God. As a young Christian seek to give God your best because when you are called it is the habits you have acquired before the call that you are going to exhibit during the call. The laying on of hands to commission you into your call may impact unto you spiritual gifts and the grace to deploy them but will not fundamentally changed your character. But the grace of God will help you become who you need to be to excel in your call. Being called by God does not necessarily mean you will be paid by a church. The fulfilment of your ministry will bring blessings which will provide for all your needs.

Hearing God from His Word

For the word of God is alive and active. Sharper than any double-edged sword, it penetrates even to dividing soul and spirit, joints and marrow; it judges the thoughts and attitudes of the heart (Hebrews 4:12).

As someone under direct employment of heaven you need to be clear of what headquarters is saying at all times. One of the media the spirit of God will use is the Word of God. A passage will suddenly jump at you, though you might have read it several times in the past. The understanding the Holy Spirit will give you of the text will be just the answer you needed to move forward in life. When God calls you, he sets before you a vision or an objective to fulfil. It is therefore necessary to have feedback from Him to assure you that you are still on track. If you are within your call before marriage it will aid you in knowing what partner will be suitable for you instead of just deciding based on physical attraction. However, many receive the call of God and never go back to him for further instructions: they continue with their own ideas and keep believing they are pleasing the master who called them.

Hearing God in Your Heart

My sheep listen to my voice; I know them, and they follow me (John 10:27).

Because our God is incredibly inventive and requires complete obedience, he will sometimes change the medium of communication to ensure that he has our full attention. Just as the devil speaks to our heart so distinctly that we are not confused as to what temptation to yield to; God also speaks to our hearts in an unmistakably clear manner. I used to wonder when people talked of making life decisions based on what God said in their hearts. I questioned if they thought it up or heard wrong. But I have realised that when God speaks in your heart it is as compelling us knowing just by a glance weather a lady will make a good partner. Without talking, verifying or even speaking to her: it is settled in your heart. The Bible says Jonathan's soul was tied to David just upon hearing him talk for the first time to his father the king. No one will make a life changing decision on a passing thought and say the Lord said so. So do not ignore the unmistakeable power of God.

Faithful witness

"*Moses was faithful as a servant in all God's house,*" *bearing witness to what would be spoken by God in the future* (Hebrews 3:5).

Strive to be faithful to God as Moses was. Throughout your ministry as an instrument of God, He will send people to speak to you. They may be matured Christians, they might even be people who are not in the faith to confirm what he has told you already or to remind you of something you failed to hear or are ignoring. So long as you are God's sheep he will speak to you by any means necessary. When Balaam ignored

His many warnings he spoke through a donkey. Do not listen to the advice of your friends above the counsel of the Lord and you will prosper in everything you do.

Committing all your ways to the lord

Trust in the Lord with all your heart and lean not on your own understanding; in all your ways submit to him, and he will make your paths straight (Proverbs 3:5-6)

Above all learn to put things before the Lord before you start working at them. The Bible admonishes us to trust in the Lord and not to lean on our own understanding. In all your ways acknowledge God and he shall direct your path. Set your inspired plans before the lord in fasting and prayer and he will give you the desires of your heart. We as men plan with some history and experience serving as guide but the Lord instructs with eternity in view. Trust the Lord at all times and He will be with you through thick and thin. As you submit to the Lord all your ways the world will submit to you. As you hear and obey the Lord: the world will hear of you.

After learning to hear from God you need to acquire skills which will make you relevant in today's technological era. You will need to learn to deploy tools which can help put your shining light on the hill of the internet for the world to see. The next chapter will teach you how to do that.

GOLD NUGGETS

Knowing how to live according to God's purpose for my life
1) To have the grace of God to go far in life you need to know the will of God for your life.
2) The best you can be is what God made you to be: as you live according to his will all the gifts and talents work together to announce you to the world.
3) God's word is sharp and active let it speak to your own situation: let it cut down all the evils planted in your life by deeds or association.
4) A man or woman after God's heart is the person whose every step is ordered of the Lord. Learn to move only by His prompting or direction.

HABIT 12: CODING

Learning Microsoft Office Suite

I attended one of the best secondary schools in Ghana and when it came to science we were consistently in the first ten in the country. However in the late 90's computer was still rare in our school. Our school hosted the science resource centre in the entire Kwahu South district in the Eastern Region at the time. The kwahu South district now encompasses several political districts.

Hence we had the privilege of being provided with computers. But most of them were covered and kept away from students because teachers thought we will destroy them if they were used. I saw a computer for the first time in this science resource centre and we were not even allowed to touch it. But its complexity was not lost on me: I thought to myself 'a machine that can play videos and music at the same time.' Wow!

I therefore decided to learn Microsoft office suit upon entering university. Because even at the university computer was still rare and we were only doing theory. This knowledge I acquired helped me a lot through the course, scoring over eighty percent with ease. In fact I dated my wife using the internet because she was in another university. If the learning of Microsoft office suite could aide me to find a wife then consider what learning how to code would help you achieve in a world that is becoming more digital by the day.

Coding

Coding is the process of designing, writing, testing, debugging / troubleshooting, and maintaining the source code of computer programs. A source code is any collection of code, possibly with comments, written using a human-readable programming language, usually as plain text. The source code of a program is specially designed to facilitate the work of computer programmers, who specify the actions to be performed by a computer. Coding is the set of instruction we give a computer to follow to achieve set objectives (Wikipedia, 2018)[29]. More and more mundane things are becoming 'smart' or in plain language programmable. From roads to household gadgets are all being programmed to perform additional functions automatically. A young person who wants to excel must know some programming so as to handle these smart everyday devices for optimum utilisation. Can you imagine that something as trivial as drying pegs are being programmed?

Writing of programing language

In time past the illiterates of society were those who could not read or write. Such people were seen us liabilities to society because they could only learn from experience. Learning by experience is often costly and extremely slow: because every example has to be demonstrated and there is very little room for self-tuition. The countries which manage to get substantial numbers of their people learning to read and write took the commanding heights of the global trade at the time. Because their ability to learn and pass knowledge through books was raised exponentially.

People could suddenly learn from people in countries they have never met: students could learn the forty years' experience of someone in just one page of reading. Scholars could suddenly pass their findings from their experiments to several hundred students who could then build on it to make more findings. Here the mantra that 'knowledge is Power' became real. The greatest cities at the time also had the most books or schools.

The nations which were late in having literate societies lagged behind and were subsequently subjugated by the more learned ones for centuries. The development gap in the world is not a race gap but a knowledge gap. Another opportunity has once again come after the era of brute force; then that of knowledge to the digital era and only a society that is vested in coding will take the commanding heights of the worlds' economy. If you want to matter in ten to twenty years' time, you will need to know how to code.

Internet of things

The knowledge of how our future world is going to work will all be based on knowing how to code. Cars will be talking to each other as well as other appliances in your house. Your ability to verify if what is been communicated is accurate will depend on your understanding of programming. Just as we take written text for granted on our street now, coding will be that common in the near future. Those who are great at this skill have already started topping as some of the most powerful people in the world and will even be greater in the near future. Great coding will make up for the power of multitudes and help make accurate most of the mistakes we commit as human beings because of the flaws of tiredness. Already coding schools are being established in many developing countries to try and leapfrog the industrialised era over hundred years ago.

Media and commerce in general is moving to the internet at a very fast pace. Many brick and mortar businesses are gradually relocating to the net for a global reach. We now have a 'digital divide' instead of just a poverty divided. Government agencies are moving at a fast pace to the net to provide all inclusive services. Knowledge is increasing at a dizzying rate on the internet.

Buckminster Fuller created the "Knowledge Doubling Curve"; he noticed that until 1900 human knowledge doubled approximately every century. By the end of World War II knowledge was doubling every 25 years. Today different types of knowledge have different rates of growth. For example, nanotechnology knowledge is doubling every two years and clinical knowledge every 18 months. But on average human knowledge is doubling every 13 months. According to IBM, the build out of the "internet of things" will lead to the doubling of knowledge every 12 hours (Schilling, 2013)[30].

Knowledge in itself is increasing so fast that being able to recollect facts and figures will not be considered as essential skills anymore. Unless you have the skills to build and maintain the machines which will be performing this functions in the future you will not be of much use to society. If you think this is an exaggeration, consider the fact that cars driving themselves was a crazy concept ten years ago and now it is a reality.

GOLD NUGGETS

Coding
1) Learning how to code is the 'new literacy' just as learning how to use the computer was thirty years ago.
2) Learning how to code will enable the youth to partake fully in the digital age.
3) Mastery of coding will help tomorrow's leaders to take the commanding heights of the world economy.
4) Learning how to code will be the only way to keep control of machines which are learning how to code themselves now from dominating activities on behalf of the few great programmers.

HABIT 13: SELF PROMOTION

Self-Promotion

There are over a billion people in this world and most of the time they are focused on their own lives. To be recognised amongst billions you need to intentionally take step to put yourself out there. Because once you are known, what you stand for will also be known. Let us stop the tendency to give exclusive prominence to people whose purpose is to spread filthy things.

The people you recognise and call public figures are so called because they put a scheme in place to promote themselves. These people have had several articles written about them. They have paid sometimes to be interviewed on television and radio stations. There a people who landed juicy music and even advertising contracts because of their intensive self-promotion on YouTube or on their video blogs.

"*I am the true vine, and my Father is the gardener* (John 15:1).

Jesus was the son of God from birth but his own siblings did not even believe him. But as he put himself out there and proclaimed who he is people began to buy into his vision. After thirty years of silence he burst unto the seen saying I am the messiah and I have the anointing to proclaim the year of jubilee to all those in bondage. After he gained some following he told the new converts not to be disloyal by saying I am the true vine it is only in me can you survive.

God said to Moses, "I am who I am. This is what you are to say to the Israelites: 'I am has sent me to you (Exodus 3:14).'"

The Israelites had no written text about Jehovah in Egypt: all the patriarchs had died so their knowledge of God had faded. The Lord therefore had to promote himself to these group of people who though cried to the 'God of their fathers' had little to know connection to Him. What was the best way to tell them that he was capable of taking them from the most advanced economy known to man at the time to a comparatively better country they had not seen? He Demonstrated His superiority by giving them a blank check. He answered Moses: 'tell them I am whoever they want me to be. 'No wonder even in the middle of a desert they were murmuring for meat. They believed they were moving with a God who could be everything to everyone at all times.

As a young person learn to use the language of '*I am*'. Learn to announce to people who want to impose their sinful lives on you that: 'I am a child of God.' When invited to a life of compromise announce boldly that you cannot be part because: 'I am a born again'; and learn to proclaim when needing material breakthroughs that '*I am a covenant child of God*'. These '*I am*' proclamations should not leave your lips if you want to make clear where your loyalties are in the presence of mockers and doubters.

Looking the part

Though a book is not to be judged by its cover, you will be surprised how many books are not picked because of an uninviting cover. Since you are a walking signpost, be careful what you put on that signpost because people will certainly treat you mostly by the way you look before anything else. Look confident and always weigh your words carefully because one careless word may be your undoing in the eyes of another. Looking presentable does not necessarily mean wearing expensive clothes but means wearing appropriate clothes for each occasion.

Confident mannerisms

Look in the face of people when talking and have a firm handshake. Learn the habit of introducing yourself if you need to catch someone's attention and use active listening techniques when conversing with people. Seek clarity in any conversation before you form wrong impressions about people. Be of help to anyone you encounter: nothing promotes a person better than his ability to come to the aid of people who need it.

Living In The Shadows

I spent the better part of my life after secondary school hiding because I thought that was how humble people should carry themselves. I remember dodging every post I was given till I was told I had to at least accept the assistant position on a number of occasions. I remember speaking at my final year in the university in our denomination's evening church service when many of the core leadership of the group had travelled and receiving great acclaim. After I finished with my message many people amongst the congregation had this question on their lips: where were you when we were choosing leadership? I have learnt subsequently that David was anointed as king but was still in the wilderness till he offered himself with all confidence to fight Goliath and the rest they say is history. If you know how to do something work at it and be ready to excel when the opportunity presents itself. Hiding only delays your mandate and the benefits which are associated with it: hiding talent only benefits the devil.

GOLD NUGGETS
Self-Promotion
1) Let people know what the power of God has made you in Christ.
2) Act confident because you are a prince or princess of the kingdom of God.
3) Always verify by two or more witnesses the things you hear about people before forming an opinion about them.
4) Hiding your talents only delays the benefits it will bring you and your generation when they are deployed.
5) Obscurity is not the same as humility: the servant who played it safe by not trading with the talent was called wicked and unfaithful.

HABIT 14: READING NON ACADEMIC BOOKS

Readers are leaders

One world renowned financial guru said and I agree that the more you learn the more you earn. The wealth gap is a knowledge gap: that is why most illiterate rich men who start businesses when they die go with all their business secrets. Such businesses usually die with the founder because there was no transfer of documented knowledge to the next generation. Nations which have had one businesses transfer leadership for four, five generations are literate societies. Readers of books besides their core academic books will usually have advance knowledge above their peers and will naturally be thrust forward to leadership of their contemporaries.

Reading makes accessible the experiences of others and helps the reader to appreciate the unique experiences of others. Books ensure continuity of knowledge and gives the next generation the opportunity to build on previous knowledge. A wealthy society is a learned society and it produces widely read leaders. Semi-literate leaders are often insecure and tend to be dictatorial and oppressive. Reading takes you through the life of the author or subject being discussed and affords you the opportunity to learn from their strengths and weaknesses.

Have a targets of reading a number of book in relevant areas

When you come, bring the cloak that I left with Carpus at Troas, and my scrolls, especially the parchments (2 Timothy 4:13).

Apostle Paul, the author of more than half of the New Testament was an ardent reader. The importance he attached to reading of books is demonstrated in the scripture above where he admonished Timothy to bring his books. Set targets to read a number of books every year in a subject or subjects of interest and you will be equipped for excellent works.

Reading My father's Entire Library

I was an ardent reader as a teenager. I remember reading my father's collection of books which took him several decades to gather in a few months after my basic education examination. Books which ranged from novels through to theology and on family life. I grew up in a rural area and attended a government school but my knowledge of the world through my readings gave my elite secondary school mates the impression that I was widely travelled. Some even insisted I was the son of a government minister who was trying to lie low in the school under a false identity. For years my secondary school mates thought I could not speak any local language. This was coming from people who were raised speaking English because they attended elite private basic schools and grew up mostly in posh neighbourhoods. This is what the love of reading can accomplish: the amazing power of books to transform and inform.

GOLD NUGGETS

Reading of non-academic books
1) Reading gives you access to the knowledge of others and the lessons from their experiences.
2) Reading has the power to inform and transform you.
3) Reading prepares you to lead by giving you knowledge beyond that of your contemporaries.
4) Books introduce the reader to a new world and gives new perspectives to things which are not found in his or her culture or environment.

HABIT 15: USE OF EMOTIONAL INTELLIGENCE

How Jacob took Esau's blessings

Jacob was the quiet type so his father Isaac preferred Esau in spite of all his excesses to be the heir of the Abrahamic blessings on the family. Jacob could have resulted to bitterness and evil schemes instead he chose to use emotional intelligence to reclaim the blessings he was promised through prophecy. Jacob studied Esau and noticed that he was prone to rush decision when in need and used it against him. He waited till he returned from hunting hungry and struck by insisting he sold his birth right to him before he will give him food to eat. Being rushed he did not think it through and completely disregarded his birth right and sold it for a bowl of soup.

Once when Jacob was cooking some stew, Esau came in from the open country, famished. He said to Jacob, "Quick, let me have some of that red stew! I'm famished!" (That is why he was also called Edom) Jacob replied, "First sell me your birth right. "Look, I am about to die," Esau said. "What good is the birth right to me?" But Jacob said, "Swear to me first." So he swore an oath to him, selling his birth right to Jacob. Then Jacob gave Esau some bread and some lentil stew. He ate and drank, and then got up and left. So Esau despised his birth right (Genesis 25:29 -34).

If you do not learn the weaknesses and strength of your dominant emotion, people will always take advantage of you and wreck your faith at the least opportunity. Know people's emotional maturity as you assigned them tasks or you will put round pegs in square holes. Knowing how to carry yourself emotionally will endear you to your superiors, customers, mates and subordinates alike. One act of emotional immaturity can destroy a reputation that has taken years to build.

Understanding temperament

As the boys were growing up Esau became skilled at hunting and was a man of the outdoors, but Jacob was the quiet type who tended to stay indoors. Isaac loved Esau because he loved to hunt, while Rebekah loved Jacob. (Gen 25:27-28, ISV).[31]

People have temperaments which makes them loud, outgoing, whilst others are quiet or reserve. These temperaments guide people in their dealings with their fellow men. Knowing someone's temperament will equip you to understand why he or she has certain tendencies. Understanding the tendencies of people will help you know whether decisions they take are based on emotions or have been thoroughly considered. Understanding that temperament like any habit can be reversed with conscious consistent effort will help you change many bad habits. Pick roles which fit your temperament and you will excel with ease.

Understanding Emotional manipulation

People have often used people's temperament against them and tried to define which roles they can perform well in. But temperaments are tendencies, not certainties because people often act out of character when they are well motivated. Jacob was obviously underrated by his father because he was the quiet type. Many times the loud and outgoing are seen as leaders but such people often lack a well thought out vision. To provide the practical steps to achieve a vision, they often rely on the quiet but pensive type. Being outgoing does not mean you are friendly and being quiet does not mean you are anti-social. Learn to stand up for what you believe irrespective of your temperament.

Now Moses was a very humble man, more humble than anyone else on the face of the earth. (Numbers 12:3).

Moses was the quiet type but was used as the redeemer of a very stubborn group of people from the land of Egypt. Being a quiet parent or husband does not mean you should renege on ensuring discipline in the home. A quiet person is not a weak person neither is a loud person a strong person: they are just tendencies and should not restrict you in what you want to achieve in life.

Changing Temperament

When I was much younger I was extremely outgoing: I even went hunting with dogs for game. I was always in a group embarking on one adventure or the other. When I became born again I buried myself in the scriptures and became increasing quiet and less sociable. My new found quiet nature was often mistaken for weakness but each time someone pushed me to change my principles they hit a brick wall and then realise that it is 'suicidal to take the gentle strides of a leopard for cowardice'. Unlike those loud friends with an exoskeleton; I had an endoskeleton. I looked softer on the outside but was much harder on the inside. With time though, I accepted some of the limitations people placed on me because of my quiet personality and found myself more comfortable in the shadow of others instead of leading myself. Please do not let people box you as capable of this and not that because of your temperament: you can do all things through Christ who strengthens you.

GOLD NUGGETS

Use of emotional intelligence

1) People are usually surer of how they feel about something than what they know as a matter of fact: people usually argue out of emotions and not convictions.
2) People are more in tune with their feelings than the facts of a matter: therefore do not reason with an angry or sad person.
3) Use your knowledge of people's temperament to assign them to tasks they will be more comfortable with.
4) Do not restricts people from pursing a vision because of their temperament: purpose is stronger than temperament.

HABIT 16: MEMORISATION

Memorisation

Memorisation is the process of committing something to memory. Committing something to memory is a mental process undertaken in order to store memory for later recall (Wikipedia, 2018)[32]. I believe you have heard severally that we need to stress understanding above memorisation but what the promoters of that ideal fail to say is that you cannot even speak unless you reproduce words you have memorise over the years. There is no knowledge without memory. In fact you cannot apply principals you have not memorised.

There are many concepts which inspire understanding after they have been memorised. I believe critics of memory based learning are not against it but really mean that after memorisation students need to test the knowledge memorised to improve or add to it. Dear reader do not leave this earth with all you have memorised, used it to form new knowledge to impact the lives of others.

Power of memory

A memory is a record, it can save lives and resolve disputes. Memory of something important could save the life of millions. A computer's power is measured by how much it can memorise and how fast it can process commands. Your memory is what stores all that life has taught you: the joy, pain, victories, relationships etc. Please take memory lessons seriously: they are not only for passing exams but also to give you the capacity to reproduce vital information when required to do so. The fastest growing companies in the world now are companies which have great ability to store information on the performance of products and the data on customers. Every countries level of development is directly proportional to what it can memorise or store now and recollect for future use: because a nation that does not know its past is bound to repeat its mistakes.

Recollection and Intelligence

Without memory there is no recognition and without recollection there is no intelligence. *According to Wikipedia intelligence can generally be described as the ability to perceive or infer information and to retain it as knowledge to be applied towards adaptive behaviours within an environment or context*[33]. Without memorisation maps could not be read, music sang, pictures recognised, addresses remembered and so on. Memory is the bedrock of intelligence and planning. Your spiritual intelligence therefore shoots up when you memorise scriptures. In time of distress and pressure only things from memory can be recollected to fight the words of the enemy. When our minds are tempted to do evil, the scriptures in our minds spring up as a defence. Dear reader, how strong is your memory of scriptures to fight the filthy things the enemy throws at your mind every day?

Impact of Data on Analysis

Anytime we have a feeling, whether bad or good it has been inferred from memory. Our moods and general disposition is as a result of things stored in our minds. In fact our tendencies and even our habits are drawn from memory stored deep within us. Things we have watched, heard, felt and experienced so often they have become ingrained in us and are shaping behaviours. Please learn to gather adequate data on issues before drawing conclusions. Learn from any sector you intend to serve as a worker or business owner. Having comprehensive data on people, policies and plans and a sharp memory of people in your community helps connect with people easily as business partners or customers. Knowing people's faces and their names and being able to recollect it at the appropriate time will endear you to community leaders and people who control resources you may need. Appropriate data analysis will help you identify needs in your community and help you find business solutions to bring you wealth and influence. Do not waste your young mind on memorising lustful and violent images in various media which will immobilise your inner energy and reduce your creative abilities.

Memorising of Sixty-Six Scriptures of the Bible

As a young Christian I was fortunate to understand the power of memorising scriptures early for the guarding of my mind. Because I understood the minds of young people are very imaginative and need to be filled with good memories or evil will fill it. I come from a long line of womanizers so I chose scriptures which dealt with temptation and also spoke about the victory we have in Christ. Those scriptures always came to my mind to help me fight temptation in my time of weakness. By the grace of God I married still virgin at the age of thirty though my wife and I courted for six years.

The word of God is powerful: sharper than any two edged sword. It is an active spirit that is ready to do battle against the darts the enemy throws to your mind daily. Have scriptures that you can fall on with 'it is written' and they will guide you to all righteousness. Memorised scriptures are the surest way of shooting down the propaganda of the devil and his agents.

GOLD NUGGETS

Memorisation
1) A computer's ability to memorise is one indicator of how powerful it is.
2) The most flourishing companies in the world today are companies which can store gargantuan amounts of data.
3) Your ability to recall relevant data when needed and to analyse it to produce meaningful results is an indication of intelligence.
4) When you are alone in a corner facing temptation only the word of God stored in your spirit will jump to your aid.
5) The only way to guard your mind with all diligence is with memorised scriptures.

HABIT 17: THE PLAYING OF AN INSTRUMENT

Extensive studies have shown that children display long-term positive results from playing musical instruments. In fact, the benefits of music have been proven more effective in strengthening abstract reasoning skills in younger and older children than does teaching them computers skills. Kids aren't the only ones who can reap the benefits of learning an instrument. Adults will also gain tremendously from playing a musical instrument. Music has been shown to reduce stress, increase productivity, develop creativity, and build confidence (Joy Tunes, 2016)[34].

There are many people who are walking around frustrated because they never had the opportunity to explore the musical talent deposited in them. In most advance countries learning to play an instrument is part of the curriculum. During my schooling I was exposed to the study of French, did weaving under vocational skills and even sawing under technical skills but not once was I taught how to play a musical instrument. The idea of teaching someone to play musical instrument was thought to be elitist. What they failed to realise was that the people having this culture were the elite because of how it helps open their creativity. Every culture of a successful group contributes to that group's success.

Check the books and pictures of the great inventors and philosophers of the age gone by (i.e. the 20th century) and you will always see a musical instrument in one corner of their house or as part of the activities they engaged in as they were growing up. Albert Einstein's instrument of choice was the violin. Not only can playing and learning how to play an instrument help improve your cognitive ability, it can also be the beginning of a great career in the music industry. Avail yourself to the learning of musical instruments and the mastery of same before thirty and you may discover a rewarding world awaiting your brilliance. If you already play in church, set goals to go higher and to do more with the skills acquired after many years of training.

GOLD NUGGETS

The playing of an instrument
1) The playing of instrument strengthens abstract reason more than computing skills.
2) Playing of a musical instrument in an adult reduces stress and increases productivity.
3) The playing of an instrument can be the beginning of a great career in the music industry.
4) Set goals for the level of your skills in the playing of an instrument and with time the world will hear the tunes you will play or compose.
5) Learn to not only enjoy music but to be part of those who contribute to creating musical content.

HABIT 18: THE CHANNELLING OF MY PASSION INTO PRODUCTIVE VENTURES

Passion

Passion is a very powerful feeling, for example of sexual attraction, love, hate, anger, or other emotion: an extreme interest in or wish for doing something, such as a hobby, activity, etc. (Cambridge Advanced Learner's Dictionary, 2018)[35]. To progress in life you need to add to passion knowledge, experimentation and mentoring. When passion fully matures with knowledge and experimentation, it produces inventions and innovations. Every young person is full of passion: this passion for sports, someone or a career is what keeps you going in spite of all the challenges in pursuing it. Passion is what overrides the tendency to be selfish and empowers you to go further, stay longer and do better.

Computer games and coding

You may have passion for coding or computer games. That powerful feeling for coding or gaming is the impetus you need to master the techniques in gaming or master how to make your own games. The best people in any sports or field are also those who are most passionate about it. The computer games industry is a multi-billion dollars industry and needs passion to break through to enjoy a piece of this digital action. Do not just be a consumer of the games become a content creator.

International video game revenue is estimated to be $81.5B in 2014 This is more than double the revenue of the international film industry in 2013 In 2015, it was estimated at US$91.5 billion. The largest nations by estimated video game revenues in 2016 are China $24.4B, the United States $23.5B and Japan $12.4B. The largest regions in 2015 were Asia-Pacific $43.1B, North America $23.8B, and Western Europe $15.6B (Newzoo, 2017)[36].

Sports

Sport engages the passion of billions of people and generates billions of dollars as an industry across the globe.

Adidas manufactures footballs, shin guards, tennis wristbands, tennis caps, and workout and weekender bags. The apparels include shorts, jerseys, and training outfits. The company recorded revenue of US $ 15.6 billion in 2007, $Nike 16 billion and Puma $3.5 billion (Sports Industry, 2010).[37]

Sadly most of these supporters' passion is only limited to consuming sports and not partaking in the billions it creates every day through merchandise and jobs. The difference between the players and the supporters is that though they both have passion for the games the players are being paid hefty sums for their passion whilst the supporters have only their passion. Sports has gone digital, with games aired on the net. Sportswear companies make billions of dollars' from selling sportswear and again billions are made from viewing rights for games.

All the people in the chain along the various sections from training to airing of the sports have passion for the game but also derive their livelihood from there. You are dying for a sport which only leaves you hungry when your team loses; learn to use your passion to push yourself to master aspects of this game so you can impact it to the masses for a handsome fees. You can be a critic, writer, presenter, journalist, sport wear merchant etc. Before thirty master your sports of choice so much so, that you will move from arguing with friends to educating the public.

Dancing and drama

Your passion is not a true passion when basic things about the object of passion are not known. This fundamental flaw was exposed when fake African journalist who travelled under false pretences as sports journalist to Australia for the commonwealth games, 2018 could not answer basic questions about the games. These were migrants who had the complicity of officialdom to pose as sports journalist and so had all relevant documents. Knowing how people act when they are passionate about something as sport journalist will be about sports Australians just asked them basic questions about sports featured in the games but they had no clue. You would think that after paying thousands of dollars to pull of this scam they will educate themselves on the sports of the games to pass these basic questions. But they could not because their passion was to travel to Australia and not for the commonwealth games. I can bet my last coin that had the questions been about Australia they would have passed with flying colours.

You are passionate about drama and dancing, then you should be an expert on dancing and drama. For passion is not just the enjoyment of the art but concentration on anything concerning the object of your passion. I am passionate about scriptures and teaching so I constantly listen to those who have gone ahead of me and learn from them constantly. Buying books all the time and watching their programs constantly. So are you really passionate about dancing and drama? Then you have to be found most of the time with the things of drama and dancing. If after examining yourself with questions about your passion and you pass with flying colours then it means your passion has made you an expert. You could share your knowledge with the general populace for a handsome fee. You can train to be behind or in front of the camera. Turn your passion into a career and you will excel with ease.

The worldwide theatrical market had a box office of US$38.6 billion in 2016. The top three continents/regions by box office gross were: Asia-Pacific with US$14.9 billion, the U.S. and Canada with US$11.4 billion, and Europe, the Middle East and North Africa with US$9.5 billion (Lang, 2017)[38].

Music

Music is food for the soul. There is hardly anyone who does not love music. Most religions incorporate music into their worship to help convey the heart felt devotion of converts or devotees. But there are others who are passionate about music: people who love hearing music for hours without end. As a youth channel your passion for music into research and rehearsals, whether of singing, management of a musician, marketing of music or for forming a company to do all of the above. That passion to make music will keep you going when things get tough and push you to find the way when there are obstacles.

Your passion can push you to use digital platforms to record and market your music. Any genre of music you are passionate about, you should be an expert in it and should be consulted when there are discussions on the matter. You can learn to develop apps for music: apps which help with lyric, names of bands men and their back ground, live concerts venues, ticketing etc.

Digital music revenues worldwide hit 15 billion in 2015 (IFPI Global Report, 2016).[39]

Exercise and healthy living

Bible says exercise profited little but a general passion for living healthy encompasses more than exercise. It includes, dieting and a healthy mental attitude toward life and its challenges. There a people who are passionate about exercise and can do it even twice every day. In fact it has been proven that there are exercise addicts: people who exercise because they like the way it makes them feel and not because they need it.

The International Health Racquet & Sports club Association also reported that the total revenue in the fitness industry reached $21.8 billion in 2012(IHRSA, 2013)[40].King David son of Jesse had passion for the harp and played it for his sheep in the wilderness. That passion pushed him to perfect his skills: his love for the harp caused him to play for hours every day. When he added knowledge to that skill by marketing that ability, that skill moved him from the wilderness to the presence of the first king of Israel Saul. And into the heart of the crown prince of Israel. Individuals, groups or nations who excel in their passion are those who do not just enjoy their passion but make an effort to involve themselves in every aspect of the industry of their passion. Their passion usually moves them not only into consumerism but also into production of things which go with their passion in the sports or entertainment.

This is why African teams in spite of having massively talented players and massively passionate supporters who can drum and dance throughout a match have not gone beyond the quarter finals. This is so because African nation's passion for football have not even gone past the enjoyment of the game to the making or designing of even foot balls. Passion is a fuel for innovation and discovery, use it!

Relationship and friendship

There are people who cannot be alone, people who enjoy the company of others so much that they need a partner or friends by all means. People's passion for people have ended their lives prematurely. Peoples' passion for the body of a woman has landed them in prison. When it comes to people be careful what feeling you harbour about them because a passionate anger can land you in prison or ruin a relationship for ever. A man who has friends must himself be friendly the Bible says. But it also admonishes as to be careful of the people we choose as friends.

One who has unreliable friends soon comes to ruin, but there is a friend who sticks closer than a brother (Proverbs 18:24).

Jonathan King Saul's son passionate attachment to David as a friend caused him to preserve David's life even to the detriment of him ever becoming a king in his father's place. It is this same passionate brotherly affection of friends toward each other which preserved the lineage of Jonathan because he helped preserve the lineage of David and subsequently that of Joseph the earthly father of Jesus Christ. Learn to harness the abilities, gifting's and talents of your friends to impact your generation. Team up with the man or woman you love to minister to the world using all your hearts and talents.

GOLD NUGGETS

The channelling of my passion into productive ventures
1) Your passion for music will take you round the globe.
2) Your passion for friends will birth great companies or ministries which will impart nations.
3) Your passion will not enslave you but will rather lead you on to the path of greatness.
4) Your passion will produce awesome products that the world will desire for satisfaction and enjoyment.

HABIT 19: THE ART OF SHOWING GRATITUDE ALWAYS

Gratitude for things done

When Paul was called in, Tertullus presented his case before Felix: "We have enjoyed a long period of peace under you, and your foresight has brought about reforms in this nation. Everywhere and in every way, most excellent Felix, we acknowledge this with profound gratitude (Acts 24:3).

In life you will encounter a lot of people of authority or might; to gain their favour or to keep their favour you will need to acknowledge what they have already done for you. Learn to never ask anything from a powerful man without first thanking him for what he has already done for you are your community as a collective. Telling him what he has already done imposes the burden on him to do it again for even more praise or recognition. Never go before God with only requests and complaints but start with thanksgiving: recognising what he has done in your life.

Gratitude for things Being Done

Give thanks to the LORD, for he is good; his love endures forever (Psalm 118:1).

For those of us introverts: people who are mostly analytical and have minds which work with the cause and effect principle, thanksgiving as a lifestyle is very difficult for us. Whenever people like me want to lift a song of thanksgiving we remember all the issues bothering our lives and feel guilty that we may be seen as pretending to praise as though all is well. Opposite us are the outgoing personalities who tend to jump quickly to praise God but when the going gets tough are quick to despair.

The truth of the matter is that our very being and all we have in our lives are the handiworks of God. He has done enough for us to enter his gates with thanksgiving in our hearts and into His court with praise. Every day is the day the lord has made and we should rejoice and be glad in it.

Gratitude for things in the future

We always thank God, the Father of our Lord Jesus Christ, when we pray for you, (Colossians 1:3).

A powerful tool of prayer is praying with thanksgiving: thanking God for the lives of others whilst asking him to keep doing the good that he is showering upon them. If thanksgiving pleases sinful men then it pleases even God the more. Reminding your spirit that the Lord has done it before with thanks boost the faith of the Christian for even greater things. Thanks giving testifies of your faith in God to come through for you when you need Him the most. It takes even greater faith to thank God when things are not going as planned or prayed for. It takes even greater grace to pray when sadness is the overwhelming feeling on your heart because of a continuous period of grief. A thankful heart is a grateful heart and a grateful heart is always open to receive from the God who provides to all without hesitation.

Showing Gratitude

They were also to stand every morning to thank and praise the LORD. *They were to do the same in the evening* (1 Chronicles 23:30).

In Old Testament worship, they set aside worshippers whose job was to praise and thank Jehovah in the morning and evening. That was an inferior covenant and still they felt they need to praise and thank God daily:

not just daily but in the morning and evening. Dear reader set time in the morning and evening to praise and thank God and see all the things you call trouble sort themselves out. For our God does wonders when praised. He is glorious in holiness and even fearful in praise. Praise only serves to flatter men of renown and under the influence of praise most make unwise decisions like Herod who said to a step daughter: I am ready to give you anything you ask, even if it means half of my kingdom. Herod was under the governorship of Rome so he was therefore their puppet he therefore had no authority to give half of his kingdom yet under influence of praise he offered it. But for our God cannot be flattered but is rather fearful in praise. Hallelujah!

Using gratitude as prayer

Enter his gates with thanksgiving and his courts with praise; give thanks to him and praise his name (Psalm 100:4).

Lord give me a heart of gratitude: a heart that will be content with what you have given me already before I ask for more. A heart that will be satisfied with your provisions for my life before I even ask for more. A grateful heart that does need to ask for things to make myself satisfied or content in life. Help me ask for things because others need to be blessed not because I need to satisfy my greed. Having a grateful heart towards the lord is itself a prayer of contentment for the heart of one who loves God. Decide to be grateful in your prayers and your life will turn around because of the grace for gratitude that will be made available in your life for the awesome things God will do in your life.

A heart of Gratitude

Let the message of Christ dwell among you richly as you teach and admonish one another with all wisdom through psalms, hymns, and songs from the Spirit, singing to God with gratitude in your hearts(Colossians 3:16).

Our God is good because His mercies shall endure always. Not when things are great and every prayer is getting answered but when we are pressed from every side. No amount of suffering on earth is anywhere near the suffering he saved us from in the lake of fire. And no enjoyment on earth is remotely near to the enjoyment in heaven. We have every cause, to make melodies in our heart to God. Melodies extolling all his benefits towards us. Make melodies telling the devil that he has nothing on us because we are firmly in the embrace of our Lord. A thousand may fall at our left and ten thousand at our right hand but only with our eyes indeed, will we seed the reward of the wicked.

GOLD NUGGETS

The art of showing gratitude always

1) Show gratitude for things done in your life in prayer and confession.
2) Show gratitude for things being done in prayer and confession.
3) Show gratitude for things that are going to be done in prayer and confession.
4) Having a heart full of gratitude is itself a prayer and it w

HABIT 20: PUBLIC SPEAKING
Public Speakers from Birth

When we were all growing up as kids we could not keep our mouths shut: especially when we saw visitors around. We were quick to share what we felt no matter who was at the receiving end. We were frank when we had cause to remind people that they were not practising what they taught us. Overtime family members who were often embarrassed by our frankness put measures in place to shut us up. Whenever we raised our voices in public on an issue we were quickly shut down and told to keep quiet. Whenever we pointed out that our parents were not doing what they preached we were heavily descended on and called all kinds of derogatory names. By the time we were adolescent most of as with an introvert demeanour had become too afraid to speak our minds in public. Our ability to speak as children in public was assassinated on the altar of convenience of relatives.

Most children start us public speakers and end up too afraid to even express themselves: so fearful they do not speak out even after they have been abused. No revolution has been successful without a powerful public speakers to inspire the troops. Every great general or king was also a great orator or motivational speaker in ancient times. For people to run to their death in battle you needed to inspire them to reach out to their ideals, hence the need to tell the troops why they are fighting. Ideals of belonging to a great nation and fighting for the protection of those they love above their own lives prepares the troops to lay down their lives. And that is usually achieved by some powerful public speaking skills which makes the troops see this big picture.

Why you need to be a Public Speaker

Your influence on society will be limited till you harness your public speaking skills. Sell your vision to many even to multitudes through a powerful well thought through communication medium to your audience. Every powerful speaker learns to connect to his or her audience by identifying with their challenges and echoing their preferred solutions. Speak to people's heart and not their minds: talk about things they love and hate. Empower them with your utterances and conduct yourself in a manner to show empathy for their concerns as though you are one of them and the sky will be a launch pad and not your limit as to how high you can climb in achieving your goals in life. Take up courses which involves speaking in front of an audience, find opportunities in school or at work and build up from there. Remember everything good is learnable so long us you have the right teachers and the patience to practice until perfection is achieved.

Growing Followers

Always speak about things you are passionate about: the audience soon senses when you are not into what you are saying and will not be captivated by your speeches. Learn to be honest in a loving way in your speeches and acknowledge the people present for the help they have offered you and you will gain more followers. Demonstrate how through your messages lives have changed or victories have been won. Talk about the people have been helped through your messages and your audience will grow more loyal to you. Loyal followers will spread your ideas and also become vision enablers who will do the 'leg work' in achieving your vision. To be a leader you need followers and to keep followers you need to win their hearts. To win their heart you need to speak to them. You will need followers in ministry, political office, in the workplace or even as a tradition leader.

Goliath Terrified the Israelites

Goliath stood and shouted to the ranks of Israel, "Why do you come out and line up for battle? Am I not a Philistine, and are you not the servants of Saul? Choose a man and have him come down to me. If he is able to fight and kill me, we will become your subjects; but if I overcome him and kill him, you will become our subjects and serve us." Then the Philistine said, "This day I defy the armies of Israel! Give me a man and let us fight each other." On hearing the Philistine's words, Saul and all the Israelites were dismayed and terrified (1 Samuel 17:8-11).

Goliath's speech and not his structure terrified the Israeli armies to the extent that all the mighty warriors in the army hid themselves for forty days. Remember dear reader that no one talked about how unique this giant was because they had known his existence and that of his ancestors for centuries. Remember the story of the spies and the giants in the land? The problem with this giant however was that he was also an effective public speaker who knew how to appeal to the fears of the Israelites. And he almost succeeded till an even better public speaker showed up.

David's fire for fire

David said to Saul, "Let no one lose heart on account of this Philistine; your servant will go and fight him. "Your servant has killed both the lion and the bear; this uncircumcised Philistine will be like one of them, because he has defied the armies of the living God. The Lord who rescued me from the paw of the lion and the paw of the bear will rescue me from the hand of this Philistine (1 Samuel 17:32-37)."

With this speech David took the destiny of a whole nation into his hand: a mere boy who had not even joined the army yet. David knew that the only way to deal with a terrifying speech is to give an even more empowering speech. He shouted: this man will die because he has spoken against the armies of the living God. David using just words reduce Goliath from a terrifying giant to 'this Philistine'. He so run him down with his mouth that at a point Goliath began to thinks less of himself: he then ask am I a dog that you come at me with a catapult? Such is the power of words when spoken to a crowd. Learn to harness this power and it will take you to places you never dreamt of.

Young woman or man reading this start now, there is no time to waste, make your mistakes and learn from them and by the time you are thirty something you will be a force to reckon with in the world when it comes to performance in your field of endeavour. See you at your best!

GOLD NUGGETS

Public Speaking

1) You are a born public speaker, please do not let unfavourable circumstances kill it.
2) Public speaking helps you win followers and vision enablers so do not play with that ability.
3) When the devil speaks terror in our life we should speak boldness back to destroy his plans.
4) Speak grace and godliness into the lives of your audience and they in time will give you all you need.

DECISION PAGE

If you are not born again the promises in this book cannot be your portion because they are meant for those redeemed by the Lamb of God who takes away the sins of the world. If after reading this book you want to be born again say these words aloud wherever you are right now and Jesus will come and live in your heart.

Dear Lord Jesus forgive me for all my sins and cleanse me with your precious blood shed on the cross of Calvary. I forsake all my past evil deeds and plead that you take me and make me part of the family of God. Remove from me any curse that is following me because of my bloodline and link me to the blessings of the children of Abraham. I promise to obey and follow you all the days of my life. Please baptise me with the Holy Spirit and with power for the Christian walk.

Amen.

If you prayed the prayer above aloud then Congratulations! You are now a born again Christian and a child of God. If you are not in any church find a well-established church which believes in the baptism of the Holy Spirit with the evidence of speaking in tongues and commit to it with all your strength, gifts and talents.

Please write to me and tell me how this book has impacted your life to the following addresses

C/O TIDD/Forestry Commission

Box 783

Takoradi

Western Region, Ghana

Email Address: lexgyi@yahoo.com or lexgyi@gmail.com

Lexgyi.blogspot.com

Instagram: lexgyi

Facebook:lexgyi@yahoo.com

Youtube: Alexander Gyimah Agyemang

OTHER BOOKS BY THE AUTHOR

1) Fear versus Faith
2) 15 Things I Wish I Had Mastered By Age 30 For Maximum Achievement
3) 5 Things I Wish I Had Mastered By Age 30 For A Life Of Excellence
4) But Turning sinking Sand into Stepping stones

BIBLIOGRAPHY

1 Power © 2018 Merriam-Webster, Incorporated

Strong-Lite Dictionary.

2 Butler, Gillian; Hope, Tony. Managing Your Mind: The mental fitness guide.

Oxford Paperbacks, 1995.

3 Definition of Habituation. Merriam Webster Dictionary. Retrieved on August 29, 2008.

4 Andrews, B. R. (1903). "Habit". The American Journal of Psychology.

University of Illinois Press. 14 (2): 121–49.Doi: 10.2307/1412711. ISSN 0002-9556.

JSTOR 1412711 – via JSTOR.

5 "Habituation." Animalbehavioronline.com. Retrieved on August 29, 2008.

The Power of Habits.

6 Merenda, P. F. (1987). "Toward a Four-Factor Theory of Temperament and/or Personality". Journal of Personality Assessment. 51: 367–374

7 INDY Life Newsletter@ kashmira gander, Wednesday 23 December 2015 10:46 GMT.

8 WHO@2018, Obesity and overweight 18 October 2017.

9 Nurs Health Sci. Author manuscript; available in PMC 2016 Dec 1 Published in final edited form as: Nurs Health Sci. 2015 Dec; 17(4): 467–475. Published online 2015 Jun 18. doi: 10.1111/nhs.12218

10 HealthAssist.net. Habits That Make You Obese and Overweight. Copyright © 2006-2017

11 TEDx talk - Rebranding Our Shame © 2015 Adi Jaffe, All Rights Reserved.

12 Addiction: Causes, Symptoms and Treatments ByThe MNT Editorial Team Last updated Tue 5 January 2016.

13 Erik Malinowski 2011, WIRED Culture. For Athletes' Peak Performance, Age Is Everything, Culture Date of Publication: 07.12.11.Time of Publication: 12:45 pm.

14 Chris Wilson October 6, 2015, Time Entertainment. This Chart Shows Hollywood's Glaring Gender Gap © 2017 Time Inc.

15 Martha Stewart, 20 Amazing Things about the Human Body© Copyright 2018, Living Omni media, Inc. All rights reserved.

16 Dan Moren December 30, 2014; 7 Surprising Biometric Identification Methods everything from your smell to your ears can

be used to prove who you are, Technology© 2018 Popular Science. A Bonnier Corporation Company.

17 Oxford University Professor Robin Dunbar, His findings, based on his theory 'Dunbar's number', developed in the 1990s.

18 Ecclesiastes 11:1-4 New King James Version (NKJV)

19 Genesis 30:29:32 New King James Version (NKJV)

20 American Heritage Publishing Company, American Heritage Dictionary, 2011

21 Ecclesiastes 11:1-4 New King James Version (NKJV)

22 http://www.businessdictionary.com/definition/leverage.

html © 2018 WebFinance Inc. All Rights Reserved.

23 Brigham, Eugene F., Fundamentals of Financial Management (1995)

24 Ecclesiastes 11:2 New King James Version (NKJV)

25 www.merriam-webster.com/dictionary/talent ©2018 Merriam-Webster, Incorporated.

26 Marketing © 2018 Merriam-Webster, Incorporated

27 Character © 2018 Merriam-Webster, Incorporated.

28 Temperament © 2018 Merriam-Webster, Incorporated.

29 Wikipedia: last edited 3 June 2018, at 14:10. Wikipedia® is a registered. Trademark of the Wikimedia Foundation, Inc., a non-profit organization.

30 David Russell Schilling, April 19th, 2013. Knowledge Doubling Every 12 Months, Soon to be Every 12 Hours

31 Genesis 25:27-28 International Standard Version (1SV)

32 Memorisation @Wikipedia: last edited 3 June 2018, at 14:10. Wikipedia® is a registered trademark of the Wikimedia Foundation, Inc., a non-profit organization.

33 Memory@ Wikipedia: last edited 3 June 2018, at 14:10. Wikipedia® is a registered trademark of the Wikimedia Foundation, Inc., a non-profit organization.

34 Levi Editor-in-Chief @ Joy Tunes April 25, 2016. What Are the Benefits of Learning to Play an Instrument?

35 Definition of "passion" from the Cambridge Advanced Learner's Dictionary & Thesaurus © Cambridge University Press.

36 "Newzoo's Top 100 Countries by 2015 Game Revenues". Newzoo.com. October 15, 2015. Retrieved June 3, 2016.

37 Sports Industry, June 29, 2010 by EconomyWatch.com.

38 Lang, Brent (22 March 2017). "Global Box Office Hits Record $38.6 Billion in 2016 Even as China Slows Down". Variety. Retrieved 24 June 2017.

39 IFPI Global Report: Digital Revenues Surpass Physical for the First Time as Streaming Explodes". Retrieved July 22, 2016.

40 IHRSA, 58.5 Million Americans Utilize Health Clubs, on the Internet At http://www.ihrsa.org/media-center/2013/5/8/585-million-americans-utilize-Health-clubs.html (visited May 18, 2013).